# BUILDING
FOR THE
NEW

**The title of the book** is based on the text: Revelations 21:5, "I am making new all things." This text as the theme of the 1968 Bolivia Annual Conference sessions preceding the transition to an autonomous church.

**Cover collage** Bishop and Mrs. Lance Webb reading the sign at the La Paz airport, upon their Episcopal visit in 1964; the new high school building American Institute, La Paz dedicated by President Paz Estenssoro; the Emaus church, one the many new congregations; COSMOS Building on the Prado; and a Mobil Medical Unit serving rural areas.

# BUILDING FOR THE NEW

Bolivian Methodism and the Last Ten Years of
Transition from Mission to Church

*To: Katie,*
*With love,*
*Grandpa Paul*

Paul F. McCleary

Copyright © 2022 by Paul F. McCleary.

| | | |
|---|---|---|
| Library of Congress Control Number: | | 2022906964 |
| ISBN: | Hardcover | 978-1-6698-2103-8 |
| | Softcover | 978-1-6698-2105-2 |
| | eBook | 978-1-6698-2104-5 |

All rights reserved. No part of this book may be reproduced or transmitted in any form or by any means, electronic or mechanical, including photocopying, recording, or by any information storage and retrieval system, without permission in writing from the copyright owner.

Any people depicted in stock imagery provided by Getty Images are models, and such images are being used for illustrative purposes only. Certain stock imagery © Getty Images.

Print information available on the last page.

Rev. date: 04/19/2022

To order additional copies of this book, contact:
Xlibris
844-714-8691
www.Xlibris.com
Orders@Xlibris.com
835644

This book is dedicated to the memory of
Bishop Sante U. Barbieri.

On the occasion of the 1968 Annual Conference,
accompanied by his wife, Odetta, and son, Flavio,
Bishop Sante U. Barbieri
was recipient of the award of Condor of the Andes from
President of Bolivia Rene Barrientos.

# Also to the memory of Murray and Nova Dickson

Who arrived in Bolivia as part of an escorted convoy under the protection of Nazi submarines.

Murray served as pastor, teacher, school director, district superintendent, and executive secretary of the Bolivian Annual Conference. Murray, along with Dr. Lou Tatum, died as the result of an accident on the road to

Caranavi where he was traveling to hold the fourth quarterly conference of the church in December 1961.

Nova served as teacher at both American Institutes. She was an advisor and counselor to students as well as missionary families. On furloughs in the U.S., she was an articulate interpreter for the church in Bolivia to women's groups and to churches.

# Contents

Also to the memory of Murray and Nova Dickson ..................................... vii
Acknowledgments ......................................................................................... xi
Introduction ................................................................................................. xv
Author's Note ............................................................................................. xix

Chapter I       August 1950 ................................................................. 1
Chapter II      Destination Bolivia ....................................................... 4
Chapter III     The Bolivia Annual Conference 1957 ....................... 52
Chapter IV      Annual Conference 1959 ............................................ 65
Chapter V       The Annual Conference 1961 .................................... 85
Chapter VI      January–October 1962 ................................................ 88
Chapter VII     Germany's Multi-Presence .......................................... 94
Chapter VIII    November 1962–December 1968 .............................. 98
Chapter IX      1968 .......................................................................... 145

Bibliography ............................................................................................. 153
Appendix I      Missionary Personnel from the U.S. ....................... 165
Appendix II     Presidents of Bolivia ................................................. 169
Appendix III    United States Ambassadors to Bolivia ..................... 171
Appendix IV     Headlines Stories of World Events of
                Significance from 1960 through 1969 ..................... 173
Appendix V      Electoral History of the MNR .................................. 177
Appendix VI     Immigration to Bolivia ............................................. 179
Appendix VII    Population Growth .................................................. 181
About the Author ..................................................................................... 183

# Acknowledgments

This book would not have come to fruition without the help of many people. The following is a partial listing of the many who, in one form or another, have contributed to this document.

At the top of the list of contributors to this book should be Margaret Dickson. Maggie made available very valuable correspondence between her father, Murray Dickson, and Bishop Sante U. Barbieri for the years 1957–1961 when Murray served as executive secretary of the conference. Her assistance continued with documents and books filled with information difficult or impossible to locate elsewhere. Born in Bolivia, a love for Bolivia flows in her veins and lodges in her heart.

Her mother, Nova Dickson, authored a book of short, pithy vignettes of life in Bolivia. Her personality and good humor shine through every page of her book. She is joined by others who deserve our genuine thanks as well, among whom is Natalie Barber who wrote so cogently about her family's experiences in Chile and in the U.S., as well as Bolivia.

One of the first wives of several to write extensively was Bessie Beck whose history of medical work in Bolivia is the best record of its beginning.

Marilyn Hamilton's articulate expression of people and conditions, especially among the Aymara, adds a special dimension to the history.

Patricia Peacock and Darlus Schoonover added more dimensions to the historical record with books about agriculture in Eastern Bolivia and forestry on the Altiplano, respectively.

I had the fortunate benefit of firsthand contact with Dr. Lindsay Smith who provided information about the Methodist Hospital which he directed for several years.

When memory faltered, consultation with LeGrand Smith provided a source for more accurate information.

Special thanks are due to Joyce Hill, who I called on from time to time for names and other information of which she was aware as having been area secretary for the Board of Missions.

Among the male authors whose books provided basic information about the very early years of Methodist work was Corwin Hartzell, who served for twenty-six years, from 1906 to 1934. This material predates the years under study but provided insightful information about the startup years.

A key biography of Murray Dickson was the well-researched and well written one by Jim Palmer.

Those who made Bolivia the object of study are numerous and have added greatly the information about the conditions in a developing country. Bessie Beck ranks among the first in this group also with her study on the social change among American Institute students—one of the few studies done about students.

Among several contributing valuable research studies was Wilson Boots's whose dissertation on the mission approach of three groups offered insight into Protestantism in Bolivia.

Henry Perry, from his position at John Hopkins University, was able to conduct significant public health research projects on conditions in Bolivia epaxially affecting children.

Marshall Martin, from a faculty position at Purdue University, continued his vocational interests in agricultural economics.

Also, Lesli Hoey, University of Michigan, has produced useful research on Bolivia.

I have been grateful for the communications with these persons, and with the insights they have shared about social conditions in Bolivia. It is impossible to measure the impact this research has had on focusing attention and guiding resources to efforts that result in the greater benefit.

The children of missionaries, such as Maggie, when aware of my writing project were forthcoming with family information, unpublished documents, pictures, and out of print books. These were materials whose value could not be estimated.

I cannot begin to express my genuine appreciate for their interest and assistance. One has to begin with David Marshall who have been the leader in preserving the Bolivian heritage among the missionary kids.

Gary Nathan Fritz came forward immediately, lending books I was having difficulty finding, then answering questions about his parents' contribution to the educational work.

My deep gratitude to Patricia Robinson Raymond who provided documents and very helpful contacts with other MKs.

I am especially grateful beyond words for Etelvina Marconi who was our office secretary during my years in La Paz. I was constantly amazed at the work she could accomplish with such primitive office equipment.

For the many others I have failed to mention, an apology. Faces and names flow across my mind regularly and bring the wish I could revisit our time together.

I am indebted to several archivists for the rapid support they offered. Especially helpful were Ms. Frances Lyons, reference archivist, General Commission Archives and History, Drew University, for materials from the files of the Board of Global Ministries, Madison, New Jersey; and Ms. Lori Wise, archivist for the Mennonite Central Committee, Akron, Pennsylvania, for copies of the annual report concerning the work of volunteers in Bolivia, as well as the history of the alternate service program known as PAX.

Special thanks are due to Robert Auer, good neighbor and good friend. Bob came to my rescue more times than can be counted for technical problems with my computer due to my clumsy fingers. Bob was a lifesaver in recovering lost files, which I should have backed up, and in deleting floating blank spaces that appeared with the wrong touch of a key. Bob ranks high in my book for all his kindness and patience demonstrated countless times.

I have especially been assisted by Rachel Mary who has been available consistently and unstintingly throughout the writing process. I am indebted to her for reading the entire manuscript with a critical eye, as well as providing technical help in imbedding the pictures into the text. Without her constant assistance, this book might not have been produced.

My children contributed more to this book than to any previous one. I have enjoyed our conversations about the years we spent in Bolivia, and what it has contributed to the years since. Without their support and understanding then, life would have been far different. With it now, it has served as an encouragement to share with you what it has meant for us to respond to God's call to go to Bolivia.

This book begins with the incident of my attending a briefing by Bishop Barbieri while a student at Garrett Seminary, Evanston, Illinois. It covered the span of time which ended when I bade him and Odetta farewell at the El Alto Airport, La Paz, Bolivia, some twelve years later. This brief note is an inadequate conveyance of my profound gratitude to all of those who so enriched our lives during twelve years.

# Introduction

A number of histories exist on Methodism in Bolivia. You will find three listed in the bibliography at the end of the book. This is not another history. It does contain historical information. It should be seen as an understanding of the history of Methodism in Bolivia from one missionary's perspective.

I have read the three histories cited in the bibliography. All three are very authentic presentations of events of the past. I would encourage you to read them. The histories, in English and in Spanish, are scarce and hard to find but worth the effort.

As this is not a history, neither is it an autobiography of the McCleary family. I am attempting to provide the reader with insight into the events that took place in the decade prior to the Bolivia Annual Conference in 1969 when Bolivian Methodism became a national church.

From 1957 through 1968, I served as executive secretary of the conference. These were the transition years. The key to understanding the history of the Methodism in Bolivia, one must recall the parable of the sower that Jesus told. Jesus addresses in this parable the issue of the larger context in which the Gospel is proclaimed. The means by which the Gospel is transmitted are shaped by immediate external forces. This document is an attempt to tell the story of transition of Bolivian Methodism within the context of the external forces that shaped it from 1957–1968.

As missionaries, our goal was to work alongside Bolivians in setting up an autonomous national church. We, as individuals and as a missionary community, labored to make it happen. The Methodist Church was maturing as an organization, moving from one stage of development to another. institution statement.

The contribution of this book to the study of missions will quickly become apparent. I write about the behind-the-scenes preparations taken to move the process forward. This is a very personal view of the events that occurred during the ten years preceding the restructuring of Methodism into an autonomous national church. Stated bluntly, it was the end of missionary dominance over the life of Methodism in Bolivia, and the transition to autochthonous organization. In using the term *missionary dominance*, I mean the control of decision-making by the Board of Missions in the United States and leadership roles played by missionaries in Bolivia.

Methodism in Bolivia passed through several identifiable stages of institutional development:

- Period prior to establishment of a mission: visits colportage beginning in 1824; Rev. Beutelsppatcher was appointed in 1903 but returned to Chile due to ill health.
- Planting an institution: 1906 with the assignment of Francis Harrington. Constitution was changed to permit other religions other than Roman Catholicism to practice. Bolivia Methodism was an extension of the Mission in Chile; attached to an episcopal area in the U.S.
- Bolivia became a formal entity as a Mission Conference detached from Chile, 1916.
- In 1939, the union of the three branches of Methodism in the United States created Central Conferences. The mission in Bolivia became a Provisional Annual Conference of the Latin America Central Conference of the General Conference of The Methodist Church.
- In 1960 (holding its first sessions in 1961), Bolivia became a full Annual Conference as a part of the Central Conference of Latin America of the Methodist Church. It had three districts. Bolivia's Annual Conference was assigned to the Episcopal Area of Buenos Aires. This episcopal area included two other conferences

in Argentina and one in Uruguay under the pastoral guidance of Italian native, Bishop Sante U. Barbieri.
- The Bolivia Annual Conference became the autonomous Iglesia Evangelica Metodista en Bolivia by General Conference action in 1968. In 1969, it became a member of Consejo de Iglesias Evangelicas Metodistas en America Latina y el Caribe[1] (CIEMAL).

---

[1] Heads of CIEMAL member churches in 2019:
Adan Rene de Leon (Obispo, Iglesia Evangélica Metodista Primitiva de Guatemala).
Antonio Huanca Corimayta (Obispo, Iglesia Evangélica Metodista en Bolivia)
Adonias Pereira do Lago (Obispo, 5a Região EclesiásDca da Igreja Metodista, Brazil)
Alfredo Alberto Alcarraz Fernández (Presidente, Iglesia Metodista en el Uruguay)
Américo Jara Reyes (Obispo, Iglesia Evangélica Metodista Argentina)
Hector F. Ortiz Vidal (Obispo, Iglesia Metodista de Puerto Rico)
Merino Riffo (Obispo, Iglesia Metodista de Chile) Luis Andres Caicedo Guayara (Obispo, Iglesia Colombiana Metodista)
Luis Vergílio Batista da Rosa (Obispo, 2da Região Eclesiástica da Igreja Metodista, Brazil)
Moises Morales Granados (Obispo, Iglesia Metodista de México, A.R - CAM)
Pedro Magalhães (Obispo, Comunidad Evangélica Metodista del Paraguay)
Ruben Asunción Zeledon Castro (Presidente de la Iglesia Evangélica Metodista de Nicaragua)
Silvio Cevallos Parra, (Obispo de la Iglesia Metodista Unida del Ecuador)

# Author's Note

Upon the untimely and tragic death of Murray Dickson, Bishop Barbieri assigned me to complete, as acting executive director, the remainder of Murray's unexpired term. For the next two months, I oversaw preparations for the upcoming Annual Conference in January 1961. After the meeting of the Annual Conference, I returned to the United States to join my family on furlough.

Upon returning to Bolivia for the 1962 sessions of the Annual Conference in November of that year, Bishop Barbieri appointed me to the post of executive secretary—a position I held for the next five years. Being a close associate of the bishop with oversight over all of the work of the Bolivian Annual Conference as well as being the available representative of the church for the governmental and other external relations for the Annual Conference gave me an unusual opportunity to participate in most developments.

# Chapter I

# August 1950

In August 1950, just before the beginning of my junior year in college at the University of Illinois, Champaign-Urban Campus, I received a call from Dr. Fred Melvin, district superintendent of the Bloomington District of the Central Illinois Conference. He telephoned me to ask if I would become pastor for the Reddick and Essex Circuit. When I consulted with my pastor, he quoted a passage from the Old Testament about the shepherd who stood at the gate to the enclosure to protect the sheep at night. I understood him to mean that regardless of my sense of inadequacy, I was being asked to be a shepherd to watch over the sheep. In his own way he was saying there were people in need of a pastor. The challenge placed before me was to learn to be the shepherd who would care for his sheep. Should I decide to respond to the challenge, there would be God's help to measure up to the responsibility.

\* \* \*

It was Friday, January 26, 1951, Rachel and I were married in the Bradley (later Wesley) United Methodist Church. We both were halfway through our third year of college. The Korean Conflict (Police Action) was going on and I had been reclassified from a student deferment to a I-A classification, so we decided to get married before I might be drafted. She was comfortable with the idea that she would one day be the wife of a church pastor, probably most likely a rural church in Central Illinois for the rest of her life. After all, she was the daughter of a farming family in Kankakee County, Illinois. She could play the piano and had a good singing voice. She could do her part. More importantly, she would be comfortable with the lifestyle.

* * *

In September of 1952, I registered at Garrett Evangelical Seminary, Evanston, Illinois, for my first semester at what would be four years of commuting until graduation.

In my third year at Garrett, in 1955, Bishop Sante U. Barbieri, Methodist bishop whose area covered Argentina, Bolivia, and Uruguay, visited the campus. An announcement was made that he would meet with anyone interested in mission work in one of the classrooms at 4:00 p.m. A small group gathered. As I recall, it was less than twenty persons.

I went probably more from what he would talk about than any real interest in being a missionary. Bishop Barbieri was one of the five presidents of the World Council of Churches, articulate in five languages, and had written already over thirty books. He lived in Buenos Aires—one of the great cosmopolitan areas of Latin America. I could think of half a dozen interesting topics he might *choose to* talk about. What better way to spend the time after classes? I went with interest, looking forward to hearing him.

It was astounding. For over half an hour, he spoke only of the Aymara Indians of the highlands of Bolivia. His voice was soft, gentile, and full of compassion for the Indian, who, only recently through a political revolution, was moving out of Spanish colonial, social, and economic structures in place for centuries. The bishop was looking for persons who would live among them as they moved into the twentieth century. My mind was so filled with thoughts that I don't remember any of the conversation that took place, as the bishop answered questions.

After finishing classes for the week, I returned home to my two churches in downstate Illinois. I wondered how I might convey to Rachel what the bishop had said. I repeated as much as I could remember. In concluding, I told her that Barbieri was a bishop unlike others I had heard or known.

He seemed to have a genuine understanding of the Bolivian Indian and conveyed a profound compassion for those of whom he spoke. I told Rachel that he was the kind of leader in whom I would feel confident to follow anywhere. I paused, not knowing what more to say or what Rachel would think. Obviously, she knew how I felt. She knew what I was thinking. She quietly said, "I will go with you."

\* \* \*

What follows is the journey she and I took along with our four children. Living among and working with the Bolivian people was such a profound experience, it has shaped how we have understood the purpose of our being thorough out the rest of our lives. An attempt to tell the first part of that story is before you.

# Chapter II

## Destination Bolivia

When the application process with the Methodist Board of Missions was completed, we soon received notification we were accepted as missionary candidates. Rachel and I were relieved. Both our parents were pleased with the news. The board asked if we would accept an appointment to Bolivia. We readily accepted the appointment. Now began the study of what the appointment would mean.

I soon discovered that two major events were shaping Methodism in Bolivia. The first occurred on May 10, 1939, in Kansas City, Kansas. It was the union of three Methodist denominations to form The Methodist Church. The second occurred in Bolivia. A national revolution began on April 9, 1952, lasting for three days yet introducing social and economic changes. Each event, one in 1939 and the other in 1952, forms the historical background of what I want to share with you.

To understand the event on May 10 requires a little church history. American Methodism by the 1820s had attained the dubious honor of becoming the largest Protestant denomination in America. However, it began to suffer a series of schisms. The first schism was in 1828 with a segment of the church, mainly in the East, leaving to form the Methodist Protestant Church over the issue of opposition to the episcopal form of governance in favor of a more democratic one. The second and larger schism took place before the Civil War. The result was the formation of the

Methodist Episcopal Church, South in 1844 over issues of slave owning. The schism followed the boundaries of what became the Confederacy. The issues causing the schisms were sociological, rather than doctrinal or theological. The result of the schism was a formation of three regional churches.

By 1900, mainline Protestantism, in its mission strategy in Latin America, wanted to avoid the destructive appearance of competition among denominations. To void such a condition, comity agreements were entered into around the turn of the century which assigned countries or areas to one denomination exclusively. Bolivia was assigned to the Methodist Episcopal Church or the northern branch.

> In 1879, Jose Mongiardino, a Bible colporteur from Argentina, visited Bolivia. He was murdered, and his Bibles were burned. In 1883, Andrew Milne and Francisco Penzotti visited Tupia, Sucre, Oruro, and La Paz, Bolivia. *Penzotti* returned in 1884 for another successful trip. In 1906, Francis Harrington, a teacher in the Methodist school in Iquique, Chile, rode a donkey to La Paz to begin the Methodist Church in Bolivia.

Interestingly enough, of the three, it was the Methodist Protestant Church—the smaller and more democratic of the three—that took the initiative in the talks to bring Methodism back together. By the 1930s, conversations that had been going on for years became more serious.

> Francisco Penzotti, the Bible colporteur from Argentina, visited Ecuador in 1885. That would have been after two successful trips to Bolivia. In 1893, Methodist work in Latin America was formed into one Annual Conference, with Ecuador as part of the Peru District. A revolt in 1895 by General Eloy Alfaro reduced the influence of the Roman Catholic Church. In 1900, the Rev. and Mrs. Harry Compton stayed a short time and established the first public normal school in Ecuador. In 1916, the Pan-American Congress on Cooperation assigned comity agreements. By such an agreement, Ecuador was assigned to the Methodists. But due to the stress of World War I, the Methodist Episcopal Church (the northern branch) withdrew from Ecuador. In 1943, four denominations formed the United Andean Mission, and the Methodists were asked to join. The Board of Missions indicated that it was unable to make any additional commitments. A choice had been made between Bolivia and Ecuador. The Board was not able to do both.

In 1939, the Uniting Conference was held in Kansas City, Missouri, in which the three bodies—Methodist Episcopal Church, North and South, Methodist Protestant Church—came together to form The Methodist Church.[2] With the Union of 1939, all mission work of the three churches converged under the aegis of the Methodist Board of Missions.

At the time of union, The Methodist Mission in Bolivia, under northern Methodism, was increasingly in a financial crisis. The history written by the History Society of the Mission reported:

> During the school year of 1938 the buildings of both institutes were in a very bad condition. It was agreed that the two directors, Earl S. Bell and the Rev. LeGrand Smith, should dedicate their furlough year, 1939, in an attempt to raise funds in the United States for the material improvement of the schools.[3]

---

[2] The new denomination was still episcopal in form, but the authority of the bishops reduced and *episcopal* dropped from the name.

[3] P. 125, Historia de Bolivia, Historical Society.

With the advent of WWII[4] in Europe in August, the Board of Missions decided against any widespread effort to raise funds for the schools in Latin America in anticipation of greater needs coming from Europe.

It must have appeared to be a very bleak future in 1940 when Bell and Smith returned to Bolivia and informed the other missionaries of the news. This meant at least five more years with few repairs.[5]

This was not the beginning but the continuation of a long period of drought for the Bolivia mission. The Great Depression that began in 1929 seriously impaired the ability of American Methodism to continue what had been begun with its centenary program to follow up on World War I.

> The period of world depression and the Chaco War between Bolivia and Paraguay between 1931 and 1935 were troublesome years for both institutes and the church. Missionary forces were reduced to a minimum. They were the years when the expressions of "No lights" "No water" and "No funds" were too common. The "no funds" words were the hardest because they were too true for both the institutes and church work which, though diminished, did continue.[6]

In 1929, John Washburn of the Methodists and Rev. Wintemute of the Canadian Baptists attended a conference on cooperation in Latin America in Montevideo.

---

[4] Germany's invasion of Poland on September 1, 1939, is considered the beginning of WWII which involved over one hundred million persons from thirty countries.

[5] A resident of Friendship Village was born of missionary parents in Poland. While her family was in the States on furlough in 1929, they were informed there were no funds to send them back to Poland when the furlough ended.

[6] Op. cit. p. 70

> John Washburn was the first director of the American Institute in Cochabamba. He was also appointed superintendent of the Methodist Mission in Bolivia. Though he was the one who turned over the Spanish work to the Canadian Baptists reducing the congregational outreach of Methodist work to Aymara-speakers, other missionaries seemed to see him as more socially-oriented toward serving the middle-class society.

As a result, they returned to Bolivia with an agreement between them that the Methodists would focus on educational work, while the Canadian Baptists would conduct the work with congregations. Methodism relinquished its Spanish work in La Paz and Cochabamba to the Baptists. The Methodist mission focused on education. The only congregations the Methodists continued were among the ethnolinguistic Aymara living on the Altiplano in the Andean mountains and in La Paz.

The school in Cochabamba was in several locations in the downtown area on and around Plaza Colon. In 1935, the school was in such dire financial straits there was only one missionary family left staffing it. The furniture from the missionary residences was sold, and part of the school property was rented out to pay bills.

The school in La Paz, too, was in a crisis to the point of being unable to meet its financial obligations. The school's dependence on the Board of Missions for teachers meant the challenges brought on by the war would only make it more difficult for the school to operate.

The '39 Union, with the formation of the Board of Missions, introduced a reorganized structure inclusive of what had been the mission program of three separate Methodist denominations with headquarters in New York City. The union of three mission boards required a fresh appraisal of all country programs. An assessment of accomplishments to-date by the Methodist Episcopal Church–North in Bolivia since 1906 would have shown:

- a hospital was functioning in a new facility but was forced to terminate its extension to the Altiplano due to funding;
- due to an objectionable agreement made in 1924, Spanish congregations in La Paz and Cochabamba were turned over to the Canadian Baptists, leaving Methodist outreach limited to the ethnolinguistic Aymara work in La Paz[7] and on the Altiplano; and
- a school in Cochabamba operating in several locations in poor facilities and in serious financial difficulties. A second school property in La Paz was also in serious need of repair and in debt.

To such an assessment in 1940 needs to be added:

- there existed legal limitations on religious freedom. While the initial invitation came from a representative of government, it did not change the fact the legal constraints on non-Catholic churches placed the missionaries under severe restraints; and
- there was severe hostility encountered at every turn from the Roman Catholic Church, making it difficult to purchase property, operate community outreach activities, or even to hold religious services. This continued hostility, like legal constraints, circumscribed what could or could not be done.

There were external actors to Bolivian Methodism at the time that came to exert an important impact on it.

The first one of the actors we would see was the ambassador and staff of the U.S. in La Paz (some of whom were probably Methodist). The embassy was an extension of the State Department in Washington, D.C., which exists to promote US interests in Bolivia. Those interests would include the well-being of US citizens, who were missionaries, and their activities.

---

[7] Bishop William Oldham visited La Paz in 1926; the celebration of a century of Methodist work in Bolivia. One of his activities was to organize the first Aymara-speaking church as *Los Andes Methodist Episcopal Church* in La Paz.

## The Intervention of the US Embassy

In 1943, the United States was engaged in the global conflagration of World War II with Nazi Germany. The US Embassy, keeping under constant assessment the situation in Bolivia to protect and promote US interests, was aware of the increasingly critical financial situation of the La Paz school. The reputation earned by the American Institute made an important public relations contribution to the American image in Bolivia. If the school had ceased to function, a vacuum would occur in educational opportunities for middle- and upper-class children. The existence of the school became a matter of consequence to the U.S. Embassy. What was to become, in 1943, a contributing factor to the continuing existence of the Methodist work was an offer by the US Embassy to assume the administration of the school. Such an agreement would require the church to relinquish all control over the school, and the school would cease to have any religious affiliation or activity.[8] On the other hand, it lifted a burden from the mission, allowing time for it to stabilize its financial situation.

> The U.S. had already by May 1941, through Embassies in Latin America, to prevent any German foothold in this hemisphere. It exerted pressure on Bolivia to nationalize the German-run airline, Lloyd Aereo Boliviano (LAB), and turn the management contract over to Panagra, a subsidiary of Grace and Company, a U.S. corporation. On August 1, the State Department proposed a stabilization package which included the construction of the highway between Cochabamba and Santa Cruz as part of the Pan-American Highway system throughput Central and South America.

The agreement, to the missionaries, must have seemed like a ray of hope in an otherwise near hopeless situation. A burden was lifted temporarily. The school was not closed. It would be returned at the end of the agreement. It gave them breathing space to find a permanent solution. Perhaps, without knowing it, they had reached the bottom and what happened was the turning point to a better future.

---

[8] Op. cit. p. 126

The second factor external to the Methodist Mission in Bolivia was the directives from the Board of Missions in New York on what the staff thought was appropriate policy and programmatic activities in the field. The '39 Union meant that the missionaries on the field were dealing with the fact they were part of a new church. It also meant they would be living under a restructured Board of Missions in New York. Many of the missionaries, who were in the field at the time of the '39 Union, would now relate to new staff at the Board of Missions. It was yet for the missionaries to know just what impact the '39 Union forming The Methodist Church by three denominations would have on the mission in Bolivia. The first visible sign to maintain the mission in Bolivia came with the arrival of new missionaries in 1943. It was four years after the union. The board was functioning under adverse conditions brought about as WWII continued on in a state of unresolved conflict in both Europe and Asia. The staff of the board was having to make decisions based on a number of elements unknown to the missionaries in the field. One of the decisions made by the board in 1943 was to withdraw from any commitment to Ecuador.[9] At the same time, the board assigned Murray and Nova Dickson to Bolivia.[10] In the four years since the '39 Union, the Board of Missions decided to close operations in Ecuador and to keep Bolivia open.

The missionaries in the field were Methodists of the former Methodist Episcopal Church–North. The anxiety of the missionaries had been the financial insecurities of the mission. With the formation of a new Board of Missions, their anxiety shifted to legitimate concerns about the future direction of their existing work. The hope of the missionaries already serving in Bolivia was that the staff at the new Board of Missions in New York would continue providing support for existing programs, as well as commit to future support required to carry their work forward.

The Methodist Episcopal Church-South had a reputation for missionary zeal. These two events, the choosing to continue the work in Bolivia and the sending of new missionaries, occurring together in 1943 were signs

---

[9] One of the first mission projects undertaken by the autonomous Methodist churches in L.A. was to send missionaries to Ecuador. See also the articles on Bolivia and Ecuador of the *Encyclopedia of World Methodism. pp. 292–293, 740–741*

[10] P. 49, *Red Poncho and Big Boots,* Jim Palmer, page 49

for hope. The Dicksons, coming from the ME Church–South, were a litmus test of the Union. It was not clear how missionaries from the former ME Church–North and the ME Church–South would adjust to working together given the differences and competition their denominations had exhibited in the past.

## The Disposition of the Board of Missions

From the perspective of missionaries in the field, the new direction of the Board of Missions became obvious in August 1942 with the assignment of the Dicksons to Bolivia. Word most likely arrived on the field as soon as the board made the assignment. Archival copies of correspondence between Mildred Smith in Bolivia and the Dicksons in Texas as early as August 1942 in which Mildred suggested clothing and kitchen items would be useful to bring. It would have become common knowledge among the other missionaries that a new couple was coming and that they were from Texas. The new missionaries were from a congregation in Austin which was a part of the former Methodist Episcopal Church–South. The Board of Missions followed with interest Murray and Nova Dickson's adjustment to what had been a field of northern Methodism. Up to this point, all missionaries in Bolivia were members of the ME Church–North. They were not the only couple arriving in a country where missionary policy formulated in New York was introducing a transitional change on the ground.[11]

Several factors were at play at this time. First, Bolivia was not an easy assignment. The frequency of turnover was an indication that missionaries found it a difficult assignment. Second, the mission in Bolivia was going through a significant change of operation from being primarily an urban outreach to the middle and upper classes through educational institutions. The mission needed to become more evangelistic and develop a congregational-based organization. Third, the work in Bolivia had not attracted a donor base among congregations in the U.S., and fourth, the

---

[11] A delightful book to read is *My Cup of Tea* by Nova Dickson. It is missionary life from the viewpoint of the wife. Packing instructions were helpful. Page 47 tells of their quarters in the school on Plaza Colon, Cochabamba.

mission in Bolivia needed to go through the adjustment of the practical implications of the merger of three churches with distinctly different cultures. accommodating the integration of

It is important to note that apparently Murray visited Bolivia before becoming a missionary but did not specifically request assignment to Bolivia when he applied. Jim Palmer records several times Murray's choice was for either *Peru* or simply *Latin America*. Palmer was clear: the Dicksons' assignment to Bolivia was a decision made by the Board of Missions in New York in the late summer of 1942.

Because of the significance of the Dicksons being not only the first missionaries after a long period and the fact that they represented the first participation in the ME Church–South in a country formerly assigned to the Northern church, additional information is important.

Murray graduated from Southern Methodist University in May 1938 with a Master's in Political Science. In the summer that followed, Murray was involved in student activities that included youth from the northern Methodist Church. In the fall, the Wesley Foundation in Austin, Texas, hired Murray for student work. Several events were shaping his life: he heard Muriel Lester, famous English lecturer at a meeting of the Fellowship of Reconciliation; attended a student conference in Toronto in 1939 with students from Europe where war had broken out; and a had a trip to Lima, Peru, in 1940 to attend the Latin American Evangelical Youth Conference where he met Dr. Frank Beck, missionary to Bolivia, and Carlos Villapando, student representative from Bolivia. After the conference, Murray made a side trip to La Paz where he was hosted by Dr. Beck. Murray was asked by Dr. Wasson, area secretary for Latin America of the Board of Missions, for pictures and a report of the conference with no reference to a possible mission assignment.

The requirement to register for the draft became a major influence on Murray's plans. After months of consideration of his future, the issue changed from between Vanderbilt Seminary to study for the ministry or Peru as a missionary, to a choice between going to a conscientious objector camp or going to Latin America as a missionary.

Nova and Murray were married in May 1942. Shortly, they received word they had been accepted for mission service in Latin America. In early summer, Dr. Wasson from the Board of Missions, met with the Dicksons and suggested they should go to the Kennedy School of Missions in Hartford, Connecticut. By the end of summer, Murray and Nova received word they had been assigned to Cochabamba, Bolivia. September 14, 1942, they flew to New York to confirm their acceptance and assignment by the board. At the board's suggestion, they had a semester at the Hartford Seminary Foundation. In the fall meeting of the board in Cleveland, Ohio, they were among the class of new missionaries commissioned for service. They sailed from New Orleans after the first of the new year (1943).[12]

It was four years after the Dicksons arrived in Bolivia before more missionaries were assigned. Was the delay due to the war? Was it due to internal management issues resulting from the Union? Or was it an expression of cautious administration by New York which waited to be sure the union was accepted at all levels of the church?

It is not clear which of these was the case. It could have been all three.[13]

The financial situation was such that Murray, as the new Executive Director of the Methodist Mission in Bolivia, wrote that all missionary personnel and funds were applied to maintaining the two educational institutions. The missionaries assigned to Bolivia and still on the field prior to the 1952 revolution were five couples in all: LeGrand B. and Mildred Smith (1924), Frank and Bessie Beck (1912–1956), Murray and Nova Dickson (1943), Loyde Middleton (1947), and Jack and Barbara Robison (1948).

A measurement of the importance of the '39 Union of Methodism is notable in the subsequent developments that took place in Methodist

---

[12] To understand the missionary staff, see Appendix I.
[13] In a copy of a report written by Murray indicated that "the proposal by Executive Secretary of the Board of Missions in 1945 close out the work in Bolivia and hand it over to the Lutherans was a factor . . ." However, I was unable to substantiate this from a second source.

work but before the revolution of 1952. One of the ways in which this was reflected was in the personnel at the disposition of the church.

Missionaries who arrived in Bolivia from 1952 to 1955 were: Sarah Middleton (1952), Bill and Martha Kent (1950 on health leave), LeGrand and Jayne Smith (1952), Charles and Ruth McFarren (1952), Keith and Marilyn Hamilton (1952), and Helen Wilson (1953). The first five had special ties to Bolivia: Sarah was coming to join Loyde, the Kents were coming due to a personal friendship with Murray, and LeGrand and Jayne came because his parents were serving in Bolivia.

A review of the condition of Methodism in Bolivia is an indicator of the sprouting of a Bolivian church. Methodism came to Bolivia as an educational institution, not a church. In addition to that fact, due to severe financial restrictions to the Great Depression, a cooperative agreement whereby Methodism voluntarily chose to consolidate its Spanish church growth efforts with the Canadian Baptists. However, the exemplary lifestyle of the missionaries led youth and Bolivian faculty members to desire to know the source of the religious motivation of the missionaries. In essence, Spanish-language churches grew within the classroom of Methodist schools and produced the first Bolivian clergy.

The first was Moises Merubia. He began as a *(ordained or lay)* preacher in 1911 and continued until his death in 1944. Nestor Peñaranda was a beloved pastor and an afficionado de fotbal! He was retired when we arrived in Bolivia, and attended Sunday football (soccer) games as faithfully as he did church services. He began in 1914 and was active several years after we arrived on the field. Cleto Zambrana (1934) was still active after we came. There was no theological education available in Bolivia. Candidates for the ministry matriculated at the Facultad in Buenos Aires: Alberto Merubia (1944), Javier Ormachea (1951), Anibal Guzman (1952), and Adolfo Angles (1952) were educated in Buenos Aires.

These national pastors were instrumental in establishing Spanish-speaking Methodist congregations. Congregations were growing essentially in the schools and, later, independent of them. Examples were in La Paz, La Reforma and Obrajes; La Resurreccion in Cochabamba; El Salvador and in Queru-Queru, Emmanuel.

The Methodist mission work expanded rapidly with the national personnel and missionaries arriving on the field:

>1940 Hospital and school of nursing moved to Obrajes into a new set of buildings from a gift, including an endowment for maintenance from Mrs. Ruth Pfeffer by Dr. Beck while on furlough.[14]
>
>1943 US Embassy assumed administration of the Methodist School in La Paz for six years, relinquishing all identification as a religious institution.[15]
>
>1943 The Board of Missions switched support for the La Paz school to the one in Cochabamba.[16]
>
>1945 The first services held for an English-speaking congregation were organized as the Union Church by Ivan Nothdruft.[17]
>
>1946 The congregation that became La Reforma was started by Moise Merubia in what had been a teacher's residence on Calle Landaeta.[18]
>
>1946 The cornerstone was laid for the church, El Salvador, on what had been property of the primary school at the corner of Baptista and Mayor Rocha, Cochabamba.[19]

---

[14] La Iglesia Metodista en Bolivia/The Methodist Church in Bolivia 1906–1961, 113–114.
[15] Op. cit. p. 125
[16] Op. cit. p. 129.
[17] Op. cit. p. 150.
[18] Op. cit. pp. 150–151.
[19] Op. cit. pp. 113–114.

# Building for the New

1947 The dedication of the building for the El Salvador and Union congregations was held on Easter Sunday.[20]

1947 Land was purchased for the school in Cochabamba in the suburb of Queru-Queru with funds from Ruth Pffiefer, the Crusade for Christ, and the sale of property in downtown Cochabamba.[21]

1949 The American Institute, Cochabamba was built with funds provided by St. Luke's United Methodist Church, Houston, Texas.[22]

1949 The American Institute, La Paz, returned by US Embassy in excellent condition with an endowment for any future needs.[23]

1951 A school was opened in Trinidad by Helena Goldschmidt, deaconess from Uruguay, followed by Loyde & Sarah Middleton starting a congregation.[24]

1952 In Sucre, student hostel (Internado) for women was opened by Bill & Martha Kent for students at the Normal School and university.

In 1960, a new building was construction on the *Avenue of the Teacher*. Support came from the Women's Division.[25] All of these developments took place due to decisions by the Board of Missions which made personnel and funding available.

---

[20] Op. cit. p. 137.
[21] Op. cit. p. 129.
[22] Op. cit. p. 132.
[23] Op. cit. p. 125.
[24] Op. cit. p. 141.
[25] Op. cit. p. 143.

## Lands of Decision

By 1955, the internal decision-making process of the board was well advanced in planning the Lands of Decision emphasis for presentation to the April 1956 General Conference. The board was signaling its commitment by a decision assigning and sending four new couples (eight missionaries) to Bolivia, unlike those sent earlier who had ties to Bolivia within one year of the official beginning of the new emphasis. Those sent during 1955 included Cecil and Mary Tinder (1955), Bob and Rosa Caufield (1955), Bill Jack and Mary Lee Marshall (1955), and Gary and Mary Fritz (1955).[26]

The General Conference of 1956 would have needed to approve the Lands of Decision emphasis for the denomination. The board pretested the concept of the Lands of Decision Program through its network of conference-level mission structures and knew the emphasis would be favorably supported. From the point of view of the Board of Missions, the transition following the Union was a success; the Dicksons had demonstrated southern support was available; and, importantly, the first three years of the revolution indicated a potential for growth unparalleled in the past. A radical change had taken place in the conditions of Methodism from 1940 to 1955.

In the next four years (1956–1960), the board sent forty-two new missionaries to Bolivia as part of the Lands of Decision emphasis:

Jim Jones (1956), Rosa Sheirlian (1956), Virginia Bunn (1956), and Thelma Cooley (1956). Milton and Ruth Ann Robinson (1957), Ernestine Harmon (1957), Ed and Natalie Barber (1957), Jim and Evelyn Pace (1957), Paul and Rachel McCleary (1957), Robinson (Bob) and Mary McAden (1958), Bob and Carmen Gnegy (1958), John and Wanda Schmidtz (1958), Margaret Toothman (1958), Rosalla Bonoeden (1958), Bill Frank (1958), and Jim and Ellen Palmer (1958). David and Carol Adams (1959), and Catherine Rockey (1959). Gary Cornell (1959), Louis and Sidney Tatum (1960), Ernest and Anita Eppley (1960), Russell and Cecilia Dilley (1960), Wendall and Ruth

---

[26] Of the eight, at least four were from the former M.E. South Church. Perhaps the Tinder family was from the South also.

Kramer (1960), Harry and Patricia Peacock (1960), Joyce Reed(1960), Steven Smith (1960), and Carl and Julia Williams 1960).

Bolivia was the recipient of missionaries from other countries during this timeframe. From Uruguay and Argentina: Mortimer Arias (first time 1945), Ada Gaydou (1954), Dr. Pablo and Marta Monti (1956), Teresa Silveira (1958), Flavio Barbieri and Mary (1958), Dr. Enrique Cicchetti (1960), and Saturnino and Nelida Gulcheney (1960).

From Japan, Katsumi and Yoshie Yamahata (1959).

The following expansion of Methodism took place after the political party Nationalist Revolutionary Movement (MNR) assumed the governance of Bolivia in 1952:

> 1953 Land for a new congregation was purchased with funds raised by Keith Hamilton across the street from the Hospital in Obrajes that was meeting in the nurses' parlor.[27]
>
> 1954 The girls' school, Ancoraimes, was begun by Berta Vargas, a graduate of the Methodist School of Nursing. She was followed by Virginia Bunn in 1956, the first missionary, Women's Division in Bolivia.[28]
>
> 1954 A congregation was formed at the new location of the school in Queru-Queru by Bill Kent. Wilson Boots was named pastor at the following conference.[29]
>
> 1954 La Reforma Church, La Paz had outgrown the former teacher's house on Landaeta. The Southwest Texas Conference also provided funding to remodel the teacher's house into a parsonage and funds to new now teachers' residences on the campus.[30]

---

[27] Op. cit. p. 149
[28] Op. cit. p. 153, 155
[29] Op. cit. p. 134
[30] Op. cit. p. 151

1955 Parsonage for El Salvador Church, Cochabamba was built.[31]

1955 The La Resurección Church was built in Obrajes during the pastorate of Charles McFarren.[32]

1955 A church building was constructed for a congregation that had been meeting in Ancoraimes.[33]

1956 A medical clinic opened in Ancoraimes with Dr. Pablo Monti, missionary from Argentina.

It can be said without reservation that The Methodist Church formed by the '39 Union became a major turning point for the Methodist Church in Bolivia. This was marked by the arrival of the first new missionaries in 1943. There is also a clear indication that the Board of Missions was guiding the renewal of Bolivian Methodism, not by chance but by conscious decisions and firm policy making.

It should also be noted that the changing environment in Bolivia was allowing Methodism to blossom and grow. The initial change occurred when the constitution was amended which made it legal to profess a religion other than Roman Catholicism.[34] The maturity the church reached through the last great effort of the Board of Global Ministries, the *Lands of Decision* emphasis, was what would bring the Methodist Annual Conference to the point of being able to become the autonomous Methodist Evangelical Church in Bolivia.

In the politically chaotic decade of the forties, there were signs of changes to come. It was fortunate that American Methodism had gone through a significant internal arrangement that would allow it to be ready for the opportunities that were ahead. Through a revitalized Board of Missions that had been incapable of responding favorably to Bell and Smith's urgent pleas for two schools in 1939, Bolivian Methodism was supported to be able

---

[31] Op. cit. p. 148
[32] Op. cit. p. 149
[33] Op. cit. p. 156
[34] Amendment ratified on in August 1906

to respond to the national social challenges ahead. In Bolivian Methodism, a transformation was taking place from a nearly defunct organization to a renewed entity positioned for growth and expansion.

The April 9, 1952, revolution was what made possible the exponential expansion and growth. One of two major external elements defining the limits to growth of Methodism was removed by the revolution.

## The Revolution of 1952

"The Bolivian National Revolution (MNR) of 1952 stands alongside the Mexican and Cuban revolutions as one of the most significant events in Latin American history."[35]

The 1952 revolution in Bolivia brought to power the Nationalist Revolutionary Movement (MNR). This political movement came into existence in the early 1940s. Certain global events could have had some influence. One element might have been the development of anti-American sentiment erupted into public rioting in 1957. Another may have been the result of World War II pent-up feelings about individual freedom present through the European refugees Bolivia received beginning in 1939 through 1940. Most probably, however, as Alexander noted, the Chaco War was the match to the fuse igniting the revolution of 1952. It blew apart an outdated feudal, social, political and economic structure. Of the 120+ revolutions in Bolivia's short history, they had been the means to power, not the election box. As the sociologist Pareto identified, they were a circulation of the elite. The '52 revolution was one of a profound social revolution whose consequences would be unfolding rapidly. From among Protestant churches, Methodism's theological interpretation of the Gospel ran as a stream parallel to objectives sought by the MNR. Never merged, they moved in the same direction.

---

[35]  James Malloy, p. IV, *Beyond the Revolution Bolivia Since 1952*

> The Methodist Mission was aware of the conditions in which the indigenous peoples lived. As early as 1919, Hugo Wenberg traveled to New York to interest the Board of Foreign Missions in indigenous people. He arrived in Bolivia with the title *superintendent of the missionary work among the indigenous*, but with no funds. He found funds from an entity, Peniel Hall, for the purchase of a farm near Lake Titicaca. The Indians were the workforce of the hacienda system and were acquired as part of the farm. It later was transferred to the Canadian Baptists.

The leaders of the MNR were Victor Paz Estenssoro and Hernan Siles Zuazo. Both men were involved in political public life early in their careers. Paz, by thirty-five years of age, was named to a cabinet post in 1943, but by 1946 was forced out due to pressures emanating from Washington. The United States viewed the MNR to be pro-fascist.[36] Paz made an unsuccessful attempt for the presidency in the election of 1947, coming in third in the list of candidates. Siles, a graduate of the American Institute in La Paz in 1931,[37] was elected to the Chamber of Deputies at age twenty-six. Siles was a wounded veteran of the Bolivian army, having served during the war of the Chaco (1930–1935).

---

[36] During WWII the U.S. assumed control of the American Institute in La Paz. It took control of the Bolivian airlines, Lloyd Aereo Boliviano (LAB). Also, the U.S. interned several members of the Methodist Church in Bolivia of German descent, among many others, to relocation camps in North Dakota.

[37] The story was that Hernan Siles was the child of the head of a prominent family and was a resident in the school's enternado (dormitory) under the watchful eye of Helen Rusby, missionary from Nutley, NJ. Dr. Frank and Bessie Beck also played the role of surrogate parents to Siles.

> Many felt a major cause of the Chaco War was due to the encouragement of Gulf oil. In 1896, Jose Cuellar sent a letter to his brother, Manuel Cuellar, in Sucre, alarmed that it appeared the Paraguayan army had taken over a Bolivian outpost in the Chaco, an area between Bolivia and Paraguay. At the time of Peruvian Independence, Alto Peru was broken up into several countries with ill-defined borders. Manuel, a medical surgeon, concerned for Bolivia's interest mobilized a team to visit the Chaco area under the guise of a survey of medical conditions. The arduous trip back, some of the mules developed open sores for which the local guides suggested a local remedy of dark viscous liquid oozing from the ground. Lab sets proved it to be oil. This was the discovery of oil. By 1930, Bolivia had contacted Standard Oil to develop the production. Paraguay chose a European entity, Royal Dutch Shell, to explore for it. It was generally believed the competition between the two companies led Standard Oil to cause President Salamanca to believe Bolivia had the advantage.

As a veteran, he returned to La Paz for a law degree from San Andres University. As is the case in many US elections, the service record of a wounded veteran improves the possibility of wide, popular support and improves the possibility of being elected.

"The Chaco War made the Revolution of 1952 inevitable."[38] The army's brutal massacre of mine workers at the Catavi Mine in December 1942 galvanized and radicalized government opposition which took the form of a more committed Revolutionary Nationalist Movement (MNR). Other parties emerged more leftist and aligned with international movements. They were the Soviet-aligned Party of the Revolutionary Left (PIR), and Trotsky-influenced Socialist Workers' Party of Bolivia (PSOB).

---

[38] Alexander, Robert, *The Bolivian National Revolution*, p. 22

> Siles was not the only one in the American Institute *developing an interest in politics and the governance of Bolivia*. At least two others emerged as politically involved by 1952. These were Rafael Otazo and Juan Lechin Oquendo. Juan Lechin was the son of a miner from Corocoro. His father wanted a better education for his son and sent him to stay in the boarding section of the American Institute in La Paz. He was there for eight years, from second grade of grade school through sophomore of high school. More will be heard from this young man {*La Historia de la Iglesia Evangelica Metodista en Bolivia*, p. 146 fn 68). Both Juan Lechin and Hernan Siles lived in the American Institute internado at the same time (boarding section) and grew up together.

In 1951, Paz Estenssoro ran again (in absentia) for president, with Siles as his vice president as MNR Party candidates. Even with the MNR's principal candidate Paz in exile in Argentina, surprisingly, their ticket came out far ahead of their nearest rival but fell short of an automatic election for lack of a simple majority. The results of the election were unilaterally declared annulled by the ultraconservative government. President Urriolagoitia got the message, resigned, and turn power over to a military junta expressly created for the purpose of keeping the MNR out of power. The MNR had no alternative but to go underground.

Wednesday morning early of Holy Week in 1952, the MNR made another of its periodic attempts to assume government. The triggering event was, the day before, Tuesday, April 8, the ruling military junta had asked several cabinet ministers to resign in an attempt to revitalize the government. One who had been asked to leave, Antonio Seleme, Minister of the Interior, which is the ministry over the police, offered his services to the MNR in return for concessions. He was offering the support of the carbineros or police force, as his part of a quid pro quo. By 8:00 a.m. on the ninth, the MNR had control of the downtown area of La Paz and an army arsenal. Forces under the leadership of General Humberto Torres Ortiz counterattacked the revolutionaries who were mainly the police force. Seleme, viewing the response of the army, fled to Peru in exile.

Leaderless, the carabineros/police began to dwindle away. By this time, word had spread of the attempt, and loyal MNR supporters turned out in force. A pitched battle ensued with the outcome uncertain. As the day drew on, militias of miners were able to arrive to reinforce the MNR loyalists. A major factor was the militias' interception of a supply train attempting to reach Torres's army. Both sides suffered high casualties. Short of supplies, the army had little option but to surrender. The fighting was over.

The actual fighting of the revolution took only three days. Begun on April 9, it was over by the eleventh.

> "Hernan Siles asked the churches to open and the bars to close, exhorting his followers to exercise restraint. To the surprise and admiration of the foreign community, there was no looting."[39]

When the fighting ended, Hernan Siles assumed control of the government as the head of the MNR. It was said he graciously stepped aside, having served as president from April 11 to April 16, 1952, when Victor Paz Estenssoro could return to Bolivia from voluntary exile in Argentina. The pilot of the plane transporting Paz home was Rene Barrientos, a young military career officer who would become president of Bolivia. With the legitimization of the election of 1951, Paz and Siles became the constitutional president and vice president, respectively.

## The MNR Party Agenda

Paz and his vice president, Siles, moved quickly to bring needed changes to the Bolivian military, its economy, and social structure. The model for these changes were based on the example of Mexico. They neither sought counsel from Moscow nor Washington. Washington strongly felt the rebuff.

The 1952 revolt occurred within seventeen years of the devastating defeat suffered by Bolivia in the War of the Chaco (1932–1935). The military was

---

[39] Carter Goodrich, eyewitness to the events in Bolivia as a member of a UN Mission of Technical Assistance and guest at the Sucre Palace Hotel on the Prado.

a conscripted army, not made up as some armies of personnel with long years of service. The majority of the men who fought on the front lines were non-citizens. The 1938 constitution explicitly retained literacy restrictions on suffrage. The government recruited four armies but failed when it came to training and leadership. The men died as many from disease and the heat of fighting where they were not adjusted to the climate or desertlike conditions.

The veterans returned bitter and discontented. The majority felt determined that something needed to be done.

It also brought a change in the attitude of the indigenous masses. They had had their identity in their tribal community. They had tolerated domination as Aymara or Quechuas by the elites, but the war brought them to a reorganization of their identity. Through the process of mobilization into the military, the fighting, and the demobilization, they developed a consciousness about their identity as Bolivians.[40] They returned and had to struggle for a pension and support for widows, orphaned children, and permanently disabled. They could no longer fall back on tribal identity.

Between the war's end and the 1952 Revolution, congress passed at least twenty-three laws and executive issues, and at least sixteen decrees to try to keep up with the galloping inflation. Veterans' associations formed as a means of securing veteran's rights. The most prominent was the Veterans' Legion (LEC) which received government authorization in 1935. Other organizations included the National Association of Socialist Veterans (ANDES) and the Association of Ex-Prisoners of War (AEP). They had a sense of the reality of citizenship. They saw the government as bearing responsible for their condition by the years of military service they had served, and now should be responsible for their well-being with health care and a pension.

> The whole period between the Chaco War and the National Revolution was thus one of the constant turbulence and instability in government. The Keenleyside Report summed this up well: Perspective or possible sources of

---

[40] See Shesko, Elizabeth. *Conscript Nation Coercion and Citizenship in the Bolivian*, p.

investment capital will not fail to note that no legally elected Bolivian president has served out his term in the last quarter century; that there has been seven presidents and eight revolutions in the last ten years; that there have been eighteen Ministers of Labor in four years; that the Corporacion de Fomento Boliviano has had five complete changes of its Directorate in the six years of its existence; that there have been eight Ministers of Finance within eighteen months.

The instability of government and the consequential economic inflation only added to the personal insecurities of every family already burdened with the grief of a lost war.

The 1952 revolution was not the first attempt to gain control by Paz and MNR. They had made several unsuccessful attempts to bring change throughout the decade of the 1940s. Their success had been minimal, if any at all. They found it difficult to dislodge the establishment. However, global factors were entering into the national equation.

> To place in focus the Chaco War, it was just six years after the signing of the treaty ending the War of the Chaco that the Dicksons arrived in Bolivia in 1943. A measurement of the scope of impact of the war on the civilian population, the Bolivian government had raised four armies by calling up reservists—the first were those who received training (1933); the second (1933) those between eighteen to twenty-five; the third (1934) expanded to include who had been called up but due to the quota were not trained; and the fourth (1935) call increased the age to thirty-five and included all able-bodied men. Teams were sent through the countryside to search for those who failed to register. Recruitment was by impressment. No area or community was untouched by the war. Bolivia had mobilized a similar percentage of its population as the U.S. Civil War. The Dicksons arrived to a country experiencing national grief over a lost war and lost generation of its male youth (E. Shesko, *Conscript Nation*, chapter four).

The economy of Bolivia had been based on mineral wealth. Bolivia was among the four world's largest producers of tin. The quality of the ore now coming from the mines was playing out. Global demand for tin was decreasing, with one reason being the emergence of plastic. The price on the world market had dropped with the end of the World War II. Production costs were greater than market value. About eighty percent of the population lived in the highlands and were landless. The country was dependent on the importation of basic foodstuff. Miners needed to be moved to where they could become food producers. The economy needed to be moved from mineral-driven to agriculture-based.

Those who formed the MNR certainly had time to think about what it would take to bring the majority of the population into the mainstream of society. Most of those who composed the MNR came to be known as the *Chaco generation*—individuals radicalized by the war. For some, it began as far back as their high school years together when they talked about how the *rosca*[41] did the biding of the tin barons. They surely talked about what one would need to turn around a country so rich in natural resources yet actually so very poor. Once in power, they brought forward five major steps to be accomplished to reach the vision they had for Bolivia.

A. Universal Adult Suffrage, July 21, 1952

One of the very first acts taken by President Paz Estenssoro was to create the right to universal adult suffrage. This action removed requirements of literacy from the vote. The literacy rate in 1900 was seventeen percent, by 1950 it was thirty-two percent. The presidency could be gained by a simple plurality of the votes cast by less than one third of the entire population. It was made clear that the intent was that all people were given the right to vote and expected to exercise it. After this step by the MNR, it meant that all politicians had a new reality to deal with. An election to office was now based on the vote of the masses, who were basically illiterate and uneducated.

---

[41] Meaning: the in-group, the power elites

> Article 1 of the decree provided that "all Bolivians, men and women, over twenty-one years of age, if they are unmarried, or eighteen years if married, regardless of their level of instruction, occupation, or income" were to be able to vote.
>
> Article 2 provided for certain exceptions, including deaf-mute unable to write, those legally declared vagrants, traitors, false witnesses, violators of electoral laws, and defrauders of the government, if condemned by the courts. Other minor exceptions concerned those guilty of certain crimes (*La Revolucion Nacional a Traves Sus Decretos Mas Importantes*, La Paz, 1955, p. 11).

The first time an election was held after the implementation of the Universal Suffrage Law was the general election of 1956. Of the total number of registered voters, approximately eighty-five percent cast their ballots.

It was not long until interest groups emerged to try to mobilize the vote in their favor. The miners' union was a primary one of these power blocs.

B. The Nationalization of the Mines, October, 1952

The next step for the MNR was the nationalization and state control of the mines. On October 31, 1952, Paz directed the government in taking that step. Mining had been a dominant feature in the Bolivian economy. From the colonial period, the Spanish quest for gold and silver was a dominant interest, which led to the discovery of rich deposits of other minerals. Three international family companies dominated mining in Bolivia—Carlos Victor Aramayo, Simón Iturri Patiño, and Mauricio Hochschild. They avoided Bolivian control by setting up international holding companies based in Europe. Functioning as an oligopoly, the three companies controlled the tin trading affecting supply and price.

Carlos Victor Aramayo was appointed president of Compagnie Aramayo de Mines en Bolivie SA (CAMB) in 1926, with headquarters in Geneva, Switzerland. The company represented the Aramayo family mining holdings which held interest in various metals (zinc, bismuth, tungsten, and lead) in addition to tin.

Aramayo held several posts on behalf of Bolivia. About 1930, he was named Bolivian ambassador in London and followed that appointment to serve as ambassador in Paris.

In 1935, Aramayo was appointed Bolivia finance minister by President José Luis Tejada Sorzano. During World War II, Aramayo holdings contributed to the Allied war effort by producing a various of products, including tin as well as parts for weapons.

The nationalization by the MNR in 1952 included all of the company's holdings in Bolivia, including the mines and other properties.

Moritz (Mauricio) Hochschild was another of the three tin barons. He was born in Germany into a family with mining interests. He studied mining and engineering at the Freiberg University of Mining and Technology. He first worked at the large German industrial conglomerate, Metallgesellschalft.

Later, he then represented the company in Spain and Australia. In 1920, he left Germany for South America, winding up in Bolivia where he developed a large interest in mining reaching into Chile and Peru.

In 1937–1939 under President German Busch, he pushed to bring German Jews to Bolivia who settled in La Paz and Cochabamba. In both 1939 and 1944, he was arrested by the Bolivian government. Later, after being kidnapped for ransom and released, Hochschild left Bolivia, never to return. The Moritz Hochschild Group was the second company to be nationalized.

The most accepted account of the early years of Simón Patiño was that he was the illegitimate son of Eugénio Iturri, a Basque, and María Patiño, from Cochabamba. Eventually, Patiño started in mining with Compañía Hunanchaca de Bolivia, a silver company, and then with Fricke y Compañía. Patiño was assigned to collect debts owed the company store. In 1894, he agreed to accept a deed of land in compromise for a $250 debt owed by a prospector. The deed turned out to be the rocky side of a mountain. Patiño was fired and was forced to pay back the store. In addition, he was stuck with the land.

The mountain, located near Llallagua, turned out to be richer in minerals than anyone had imagined. In 1900, Patiño's prospecting led to the discovery of a very rich vein of tin. Over the next ten years, he bought up nearby mines and other important mines in Bolivia, including Catavi, Siglo XX, Uncia, and Huanuni. By the 1920s, Patiño held Chilean interests in his mining company and added tin smelters in England and Germany to his growing empire. By the 1940s, he controlled the international tin market and was one of the wealthiest men in the world, earning the title *The Tin King* (*Rey del Estaño*).

In his 2008 book *Outliers*, Malcolm Gladwell estimated the total net worth of Simón I. Patiño to around USD 81.2 billion in 2008 dollars. That amount placed him in number twenty-six of the all-time wealthiest individuals in human history, ahead of Bill Gates, Carlos Slim, Warren Buffett, and J. P. Morgan.

Patiño had been living between Europe and Bolivia since around 1912. In 1924, following a heart attack, his doctors told him not to return to Bolivia and he moved abroad permanently. He moved first to Paris, then to New York, and finally to Buenos Aires where he died in 1947. Patiño is buried in a white mausoleum high in the Andean mountains in the province of Cochabamba where he was born.

> All three men were technically Bolivians. Patinos by birth, Hochschild by naturalization, and Aramayo by citizenship, even though the patriarch, Felix Avelino, was born and lived most of his life in Paris. Only Hochschild spent most of his time in Bolivia after 1920. Official tax records show that at the height of his wealth, Patino paid only $415 in taxes to the Bolivian state.

All three tin baron families established their residence in Europe. It was commonly remarked that Paris was the capital of Bolivia.

An examination of the economy of Bolivia sets in perspective the situation the country was in 1950. The report of the Economic Commission for Latin America reported: "During the last quarter of a century minerals have never represented less than ninety percent of the value of exports and the tendency has been for this percentage to increase."[42] John Alexander noted this observation: "Not only is the economy of Bolivia highly dependent on tin exports, but the government finances have been for many years even more dependent upon them."[43] The Keenleyside Report of the United Nations Mission in 1950 stated:

Export and other taxes leveled on minerals account for almost half of the ordinary government revenues; the outcome of the budget is critically dependent in the fluctuations of the world demand for tin.[44]

Paz Estenssoro, an economist, understood well the critical position the country was in and proceeded to fulfill one of his campaign promises. Just twenty-eight days after arriving back in La Paz from exile in Argentina, he named a commission on May 13 to study and bring recommendations concerning the nationalization of the mines. As was his style with regard to controversial issues, he brought to the discussion table all of the interested stakeholders. The nationalization decree was signed on October 31, 1952.

The nationalization law was limited to the big three international corporations and affected all of their holds in Bolivia. The law included an amount to be paid to the three in recompense for their loss. The amount was disputed by the three, which led to four years of negotiations.

The nationalization of the three corporations did not resolve the fiscal problems of the country. On the contrary, it opened a pandora's box of both financial and political problems for the MNR. The MNR, now the mine operator, faced at least three problems with the tin production: the problem of surplus labor in the mines, the need to upgrade the mining equipment, and the reimbursement to the former mine owners for their loss due to nationalization.

---

[42] Economic Commission for Latin America, vol. 1, 73.
[43] Alexander, John. Ibid, 99.
[44] Keenleyside Report of the United Nations Technical Assistance Mission to Bolivia, 1950

Enough has been said to record the agenda of the MNR with regard to mining. What should be noted for future discussion is its relevance for Methodism which includes the reality of the workers organizations and the political role of unions, the plight of miners and their families due to unemployment, and the need to relocate to find gainful employment.

C. The Reduction and Reorganization of the Military July 1953

The third step in the MNR agenda was reorganization and reduction of the army that took place in July 1953. Of all the changes which have been initiated, one of the few which has changed the least over the decades is the annual conscription of young men. Historically, the military existed to fight internal battles rather than foreign enemies. Also, it tended to be an extension or tool of the party in power. One of the events that shaped the thinking of the MNR concern of the military was the massacre of miners in Catavi in 1942. The army was used by the Salamanca administration to support the mine owners in the strike by the miners. Also, many of the MNR leaders chose not to engage in exile but to serve in the military during the Chaco War, becoming knowledgeable by firsthand involvement with the shortcomings of the military.

> "In Bolivia, however, twenty thousand young men enter the barracks as conscripts each January . . . Men need military service to vote, run for office, or hold public employment . . . As is true with many systems of supposedly universal military service, they can obtain this paperwork without dedicating a year of their lives to the barracks. Twenty thousand secondary students annually elect to complete pre-military training on weekends to earn their service documents and those who want and can afford to forego training all together can pay a fee of three thousand bolivianos (out of reach for most working-class Bolivians) and many others simply go without these documents" (Goudsmit, *Praying for Government*, p. 208).

Paz saw the need for a military, but one quite different from the existing one. He sought reform, not elimination of the military. An initial purging of the command level meant at least 166 officers were removed from the rolls for political reasons. Others chose to leave. In the first year of the revolution, over half of the officers' corps was vacated. The military academy was closed. All cadets were dismissed. The military allocations from the national budget were slashed from 23 percent to 13.7 percent. The reduction in the standing army was the most dramatic. It was reduced by about 70 percent from approximately eighteen thousand to five thousand. No conscription was called for the year 1952.

> By 1956 Bolivia's economy was in a freefall. The need for external financial assistance made Bolivia increasing dependent on U.S. aid. Starting at 1.3 million dollars in emergency assistance in 1953, U.S. aid ballooned to $18.2 million in 1954, to $33.5 million in 1955.The stabilization package in 1956 not only involved the U.S. but also the International Monetary Fund. This brought with it requirements concerning labor. These obligations seriously weakened the MNR's goal for control of the miners' union (COB). Such a development encouraged the MNR to reconsider its position on the military. (Shesko, p. 164)

Beginning in February 1954, officers of the Bolivian Army began attending the School of the Americas located at Fort Benning in Columbus, Georgia; a training program offered to all Latin American countries by the United States. A favorable military policy was one of the conditions of the economic stabilization package of 1956. Paz had repeatedly rejected direct military aid until December 1957 when he relented. US instructors began teaching at the military academy.

Apparently, a distancing of the relationship between Paz and General Clemente Inofuentes, Chief of Staff, developed. It was over left-leaning in the COB among miners around Juan Lechin. Paz refused to allow Inofuentes to purge the left wing of the MNR. A letter of support to Inofuentes signed by 177 officers hardened the positions circulated. The fragmentation of the MNR became more apparent. Paz's solution was to encourage the reemergence of the military. He needed the military to offset the strength of the miners' militias and the threat of strikes.

In October 1957, Bolivian Socialist Falange Party seized oil machinery and occupied YPFB in Santa Cruz. Two troops were sent to surround the city. The issue was ultimately resolved by negotiation. However, it was the first time the military was used to maintain a *law and order* situation since 1952. In April 1958, US military equipment and arms replaced Bolivia's prior dependence on European suppliers. The military was growing stronger.

The rioting caused by the *Time* magazine article in March 1959 was the reason for Siles to call for troops be sent to La Paz. The article said the U.S. had been pouring in so much "without a d—— thing to show for it." The anonymous embassy official proposed the solution to be that the country "be divided up among its neighbors."[45] The inevitable result was the decision of General Barrientos to assume power.

D. The Agrarian Reform Law in August 1953.

| Methods of land cultivation | |
| --- | --- |
| Semifeudal cultivation | 90.5 |
| Properties worked by owner | 1.5 |
| Properties with aid of wage earners | 2.44 |
| Properties rented | 2.66 |
| Properties of Indian communities | 2.86 |
| Source: Labor Action, New York, February 9, 1953 | |

The 1950 Bolivian census indicated a continuation of the concentration of arable land in the hands of a few. It showed approximately 4.5 percent of rural landowners owned 70 percent of the country's private agricultural property holding from two thousand to twenty-five thousand acres.[46]

To the MNR, the large majority of the population survived by subsistence living, not producing for the market under the feudal conditions. It was also the reason Bolivia was dependent on the importation of foodstuff. It was estimated that in 1950, with a population of approximately three

---

[45] Shesko, Conscript Nation, p. 167
[46] P. 60 Henderson, John. Ob site

million five hundred thousand, only between five hundred thousand and six hundred thousand were involved *in the market.*

"Today, the second of August 1953, ends four hundred years of oppression . . . Today more than two million peasants have become part of the nation."[47] With these words, Victor Paz Estenssero announced the decree of the Agrarian Reform. This was eight months after the revolution. While it might have seemed a delay, there were complimentary steps being taken. One of Paz's first actions was to create the Ministerio de Asuntos Compesinos (The Ministry of Indian and Peasant Affairs). The ministry was charged with several tasks, among which was the creation of unions. These entities played an increasingly important political role as time passed. Also to encourage the creation of cooperatives as the means of creating family income.

The Agrarian Reform Law began with a short history of land ownership in Bolivia. The drafters included the six objectives of the Land Reform Law before the actual decree:

a. to distribute the arable land to the peasants who do not have enough;
b. to restore to the Indian communities the lands which were taken from them;
c. to free the agricultural worker from the condition of serfdom;
d. to stimulate increase productivity and commercialization of agriculture;
e. to conserve the natural resources; and
f. to promote currents of internal migration of the rural population.

Paz appointed a commission under the chairmanship of Vice President Hernan Siles to make recommendations within ninety days articulating the party's position on land reform.[48] The major source of dominance and injustice was the latifundio system which was the large rural farms requiring servile labor to farm in traditional techniques. The commission

---

[47] P, 3, Soliz, Carmen, Fields of Revolution, quoted from the Subsecretaria de Prensa
[48] See John Alexander's The Bolivian National Revolution, pages 62ff for a complete description of the Commission's work to create the decree.

turned to models for land reform from Chile and especially Mexico. The issue of land ownership was not of recent concern but had been one under consideration for many years. The Disentailment Law of 1874 was one attempt to redefine land ownership. Fundamental to understanding the problems confronting the commission is to recognize the forms of land ownership. The commission took into account five different forms of land ownership: small holdings, medium holdings, latifundia, agriculture enterprises, and cooperative or community holdings. The problem was quite unlike the resolution of the mines. The one took ownership away. Land reform was to allocate ownership. The mine issue was top-down. The land reform had to be both top-down and bottom-up. A third factor obvious from the start was land reform had a regional dimension: the Altiplano and Cochabamba Valley called for one-type policy decisions; and the Yungas, Chapare, and Santa Cruz, another. This had the effect of making land reform an overarching objective requiring several stages to complete.[49]

The ultimate legislation contained 176 articles. The focus of the decree was on the latifundia. It terminated the three- or four-day free labor to landowner and broke up the hacienda land into private ownership. The password of the land reform was "The land belongs to those who work it." The date of the decree, August 2, was designated *The Day of the Indian*.

The Banco Agricola was set up with a program of supervised credit in 1955.

The land reform law, along with the right for universal vote, had major impact for the long-standing work of Methodism on the Altiplano and in the Cochabamba Valley. It was not long after the Ministry of Rural Affairs was established that an office and program came into being for the development of colonies' relocation of persons from the highlands to the eastern lowlands.

E. Educational Code

The fifth major action in the MNR agenda was to remodel the educational system of Bolivia. The MNR design to incorporate everyone into full participation in the social, political, and economic life of the country,

---

[49] For an excellent statement of the complexity of accomplishing successfully the process of redistribution of land ownership see Carmen Soliz's book *Fields of Revolution*.

would, obviously, require a transformation of the education system in a country where the national census revealed only approximately 32 percent of the population were literate.

To accomplish this, President Paz appointed a Commission on June 30, 1953, to study the integral reform of public education. After an arduous process of study and debate, the cabinet forwarded to President Paz the final report for his signature on January 20, 1955.

The Education Code included forty-three chapters covering every aspect of education through high school. The code covered, in a few of the chapters, pre-school, elementary, and high school, vocational and technical training, literacy campaign, special education, physical education, private education, pre-university training, school administration, teacher training, the Ministry of Education, cooperation of parents, scholarships, and teachers' unions.

In a message to congress in July 1956, President Paz reported on accomplishments. In regard to education, he reported: in urban areas from Aril 1952 to July 1956, the number of schools increased from 735 to 847; the number of teachers from 7,663 to 9,377, and the number of students rose from 237,503 to 214,778.

International funding was needed to implement the Education Code and make the transformation needed. This assistance was found from the InterAmerican Education Service Point Four Program of the US Department of State and United Nations source.

In the assessment made of the condition of the Methodist mission to Bolivia in 1940, there were noted two serious hostile elements in the environment surrounding Methodism. The first was the legal position within which it had to work. In society, it was on a very limited scale. The removal of the first source of hostile came with the revolution of 1952. Laws were changed, and threat of functioning beyond legal limits was removed.

The second reduction in hostile threats to Methodist ministry came with Vatican II, meeting over three years from October 1962 to December 1965. The hierarchy resisted change. There were elements within Catholicism attempting to bring the Bolivian Roman Catholic Church into the modern world through their presence and work. One of these was the Maryknoll, a US Mission Society. Bishop Brown in Santa Cruz and other Maryknoll working in Warnes and Montero developed cordial friendships with the Methodist missionaries in Montero. However, the major change was brought about by Vatican II and came primarily after it was over.[50]

> The Second Ecumenical Council of the Vatican, commonly known as the Second Vatican Council or Vatican II, was formally opened under the pontificate of John XXIII on 11 October 1962, and was closed under Paul VI on 8 December 1965. Several changes resulted from the Council, including the renewal of consecrated life with ecumenical efforts with other Christian denominations, interfaith dialogue with other religions
>
> Ecumenism: Unitatis Redintegratio declared the ecumenical movement a good thing, encouraged Catholics to be part of it, and referred to Eastern, Oriental and, Protestant Christians as *separated brethren*. In 1928, Pope Pius XI had condemned the ecumenical movement. From the Council of Trent until the Second Vatican Council, Protestants were officially referred to as heretics.

The Catholic Church was caught up in the social conditions prevalent in Bolivia at the time of the 1952 revolution. While there were liberalizing elements, these were largely due to entities or orders from outside of Bolivia. Even after Vatican II, there were elements within the Catholic Church that were slow to change.

Two examples are enough to show continuing forms of hostility. El Mesias Church, a new congregation not too far from La Reforma, was the object of hostility. In 1964, a priest from the local Catholic Church after mass led those of his flock who would follow to march to the El Mesias Church to disrupt Sunday morning services. The usual practice was to throw stones on the tin roof of the church; raising such disturbance, services would have to be suspended. After this had happened several times, members of El

---

[50] Vatican II was an Ecumenical Council held in Rome from October 1962 through December 1965.

Mesias waited along the route the mob usually took. As the mob passed by, surreptitiously joined in to walk with them. In very short order, the mob was aware that now they had several Methodists among them. The mob began to dwindle. By the time they reached El Mesias, the mob had thought better of their intentions and walked on past the church. That was the end of any disruptions to the services.

The hostility toward Protestants was also toward social services being provided. The following story is provided by Dr. Lindsay Smith.

> "There were some of our (Methodist) young people doing work in the area and also Peace Corps young people there too.
>
> "As I was walking on a lonely jungle trail, I bumped into a young American, tee shirt, crew cut guy.
> He asked me what I was doing in the area. I responded that I was doing medical work, including placing some of the *Pope's loops* for family planning.
>
> "I asked him what he was doing, and he responded, 'I'm Brother Jerry. I'm the Catholic priest in the area.'
> A week after I returned to La Paz, I had a call from the government medical office requesting I meet the next day at the Ministry of Health office.
> "When I arrived, there were about twenty people in the room, including doctors, lawyers, and health official. They asked what I was doing in the Alto Beni. After discussing about doing medical work, the discussion got around to family planning.
> "Their discussion then told me my work is about *birth control* and that an American cannot control the Bolivian population, that they encouraged to make Bolivia stronger, and if they heard about me placing another loop in a Bolivian woman, they would kick me out of the country and close the Hospital Metodista.
>
> "Fortunately, I had hired a Bolivian obstetrician, Jaime Linares. So, Jaime, being Bolivian, could do all the family

planning he wanted. As an aside, the Jesuit priests in La Paz sent Bolivians to our hospital for family planning help."[51]

Vatican II brought change to the major hostility Methodism had encountered, from the priest-led mob stoning to death of a Bible colporteur in 1877 to the priest-led mob throwing of stones on a tin roof to disrupt services in 1964.

Three major changes had occurred for Bolivian Methodism:

- The union of Methodism brought new sources of support which altered the condition of the mission in Bolivia;
- The revolution of 1952 altered the political environment which removed the legal restraints within which the mission had over it as a constant shadow; and
- The gradual change in relationship just before and after the determinations of Vatican II brought to a minimum the hostile religious environment Methodism encountered on an almost daily basis.

During the first four years of the MNR years in power, Victor Paz was successful in consolidating much of the program of the party. The constitution prohibited a sitting president to run for a second term. Hernan Siles Zuazo, the vice president, was the natural successor to Paz. Hernan Siles easily won the elect for the presidency. He was sworn in as president on August 6, 1956. The political environment was more difficult as it had been for Paz. The MNR was beginning to fragment along personal lines and, to some degree, over policy. The economy was in serious difficulties. The mineral resources of the country, which had been a major source of its wealth, were playing out. Bolivian tin, a high priority during the war, was now competing with other producers' previous cutoff by the war. Also, aluminum and plastic became popular and cheaper replacements for tin.

---

[51] Information provided by Dr. Lindsay Smith, Director of the Methodist Hospital in Obrajes from events in 1971

## The McClearys Prepare for Mission Service

Excitement was building for the family by spring 1956, with graduation from seminary, Annual Conference, and beginning work with the Board of Missions.

The missionary life was just beginning to take form for the McClearys. During the spring quarter at GETS, we had worked in appointments for physical exams, dental exams, psychological testing, and filling out forms for New York. Graduation from GETS was on the seventh day of June 1956. The Central Illinois Annual Conference met in MacMurray College, Jacksonville, Illinois, where Paul June was ordained elder and received into conference membership. The service took place in the Annie Merner Pfeiffer Chapel in the heart of the campus in a service on June 10. When appointments were read, Paul's name was listed under *Special Appointments*. It read, "Paul McCleary, Language School, Board of Missions."

June 26–July 31, Rachel and I attended an ecumenical training event for missionaries sponsored by the National Council of Churches. It was held at Allegheny College in Meadville, Pennsylvania, a small Methodist school with a lovely campus. There were seventy-two missionaries of several mainline denominations. The first three days were backgrounding in general information for the missionaries going anywhere in the world. The rest of the conference was basically spent in regional study groups. Dr. Howard Yoder, a former missionary to Bolivia, coordinated the Latin America group. The worship services in the morning were inspiring. The informal times in the evenings were very meaningful in building friendships that reached over continents and lasted over the years.

August 1956 was a busy month. It was a time of sorting what to take, what to store, and what to give away. Paul took the two children and traveled to Miami, Florida, by train. The three of us shared an upper and lower berth. It had been decided that Rachel should fly down with the baby. She joined us in Miami a day later. Our flight to San Jose was on LASCA Airlines.

The McCleary family, meanwhile, was set to go to Costa Rica to begin a year of language studies. We were enrolled in the language school run by Presbyterian missionaries. The school was professionally run with regular religious services to follow the ecclesiastical year. For housing, a duplex house had been rented for us and for Jim and Evelyn Pace. The house was located across the street from a coffee factory. Jim and I visited the plant to view the way coffee is prepared for market. Then later we took our wives and children to view the process of soaking and drying the beans for shipment. Jim and I would take the bus, built on the chassis of a truck, to go to the market, on our weekly shopping trip. Everyone seemed to enjoy seeing two grown men buying fresh vegetables and fruit in the market. It gave us a chance to develop a kitchen vocabulary; something we would not probably have a chance to do in the future.

In a couple of months Rachel and I felt we would learn the language more rapidly if we moved to an area where we would be immerged in Spanish. Living in the capital city and being in a neighborhood full of language school students made it too easy to continue with English. With permission from the mission treasurer, we moved to Alajuela, a town close to but on the other side of the airport. There were three Methodist missionaries who lived in Alajuela, Rev. Jim and Glady Snedeker and Alice Weed. In addition to these three, there were only two other Americans in town.

The Methodist Church[52] was right on the main plaza. It had a colonial Spanish front. Jim and Gladys served as pastor of the church and ran a theological training program for pastors and as Christian educators.[53] This gave both Rachel and I an opportunity to immerse ourselves in the life of the church in Costa Rica, as well as the Spanish language. Alice Weed deserves special attention. Alice was a deaconess. She had a jeep she drove with one hand. Her other hand and arm were withered. That did not affect

---

[52] Under a comity agreement, George Miller, a missionary and superintendent of the Panama Mission, named Edwardo Zapata, a pastor from Mexico, to be the pastor in charge in San Jose. Missionaries Rev. and Mrs. C. W. Ports arrived within a year. George Miller was later elected bishop.
British Methodism had entered Costa Rica in 1889 through the work of Sidney Stewart, a Jamaican who worked as a carpenter on citrus and sugarcane farms.

[53] The program started by Jim and Gladys officially was named Training School for Methodist Workers in 1957. It was later moved to San Jose to become the Methodist Theological Seminary under the guidance of Rev. Marion Woods as director.

her in the least. Alice had been a missionary in China before it closed. We loved to hear her talk about her experiences. The house we occupied in Alajuela was half a block from where Alice lived with a school teacher from California. Alice was hardly home. Across the street from our house was the fire station. Our kids, especially Johnny, loved the firetrucks. The firemen loved our blond-headed children. If they left the house alone, we could find them in the driver seat of the firetruck under the caring eye of one of the firemen. The house rented for us was like a U-shaped house with three sides. There was no back wall. The wide-open space was the living room; the rooms across the front were the parlor and kitchen. On the arm of the U to the right were two bedrooms—one for Rachel and I, and the other for the three children. The large room on the left must have been for an older adult. It was still furnished with a hospital bed. Later in the year, a number of LA 3s, or short-term missionaries, came for a brief immersion in Spanish, and one of the boys stayed in our guest room. During the night I heard Jim shouting. I thought he was having a nightmare or something and hurried to his room. In the night, we had some severe earthquake tremors.

However, he thought I was playing a practical joke pushing the hospital bed around the room. Our house was rented furnished. One night as we tucked the children in for the night and heard their prayers, Leslie was at the point of sobbing. When Rachel inquired the problem, she was told that the sheet on her had a hole in it. Before Rachel to what to tell her, Mary responded from her bed and said, "Oh, that's alright, Leslie, you won't fall through."

On the weekends, I would take two of the young men from the training school to visit a town not too distant. We visited different towns going door to door, playing to gather children and telling them a Bible story, or leaving tracts for the shut-ins to read. On Sunday, we would hold a service on a street corner to draw a crowd, and then visit with as many as we could to build friendships and contacts for the next visit. During Holy Week the language school closed so everyone could be involved in a local church. Jim had a call from a local pastor on the week coast to come and help him hold services for the workers in Golfito in the banana zone of United Fruit Company, where a chapel had been built by the company. We traveled from place to place, holding services for the workers and traveling in the evening to find a place to stay.

By July, Rachel and I were feeling that we had about all of the help the language school could offer and that it was time for us to move on. We had been in Costa Rica from August 1956 to July 1957. It was a beautiful country, and the people very warm and friendly. The board agreed, so we returned home to make final preparations for the trip to Bolivia. We flew to Mexico City for a connecting flight to El Paso, Texas. From there we traveled by Greyhound bus to Kankakee, Illinois.

Our schedule didn't fit into the schedule of the annual board meeting of the Board of Missions. In August, we were commissioned in our local church[54] in Bradley, Illinois. Bishop Charles Wesley Brashares represented the Board of Missions.

The McCleary family was in the final stages of packing and saying *farewells* before departure from Illinois to New York on the first leg of the trip to Bolivia.

On September 21, 1957, we boarded a Grace Line[55] ship at Pier 41 in New York. The McCleary family was then composed of John Wesley, nine months; Rachel Mary, three years old; and Leslie Ann, five years of age. And, of course, Rachel and I. We had packed what was to be shipped to Bolivia and turned it over to the Mayflower Moving Company for shipment to New York to a warehouse of the Grace Line arranged by the board.

---

[54] This was one of the last services to be held in this church building. The church now named Wesley UMC built a new larger building, parking near the high school.
[55] The W. R. Grace and Company

> The ship Sant Lucia 2 was commissioned in 1954. It was one of six ships of the Grace Line which travelled from New York through the Panama Canal down the west coast of South America. It was called a comb ship, both passengers and cargo. Maximum capacity was fifty-two passengers. It was formed in 1854 by two brothers who saw the opportunities that existed in Central and South America. By 1954, it was entering such fields as pharmaceuticals, technology, and real estate. Later. we discovered one of the airlines serving Bolivia known as Panagra on which we traveled to Miami was a joint venture with Pan American.

## Bolivia? Take the Grace Line

We had spent several days in New York finishing arrangements at the Board of Missions at 475 Riverside Drive. We had come by train from Illinois to Grand Central Station, NYC, where we lived at the Vanderbilt Hotel at Park and Thirty-Fourth Street. We went to the 102$^{nd}$ floor of the observatory of the Empire State Building and rode the subway to Bronx Zoo where the kids enjoyed the camel ride. We rode the escalators at Macy's many times.

We boarded the Grace Line ship the Santa Luisa and began our trip to Bolivia. It was a late afternoon departure, and we lined the rail to watch the city gradually disappear from sight. The one event to break the monotony of a sea voyage was the threat of a hurricane off the coast of Florida. The ship changed course to pass closer to the shore where that evening we could easily see the skyline of hotels on Miami Beach. There would be a stop in Panama before entering the canal at Colon. Our ship had to wait in line for passage through the canal. We were able to get off for a few hours, and Reg Wheatley met us and took us to his home. He pastored a church in the Canal Zone.[56] The ship was called a comb or a mixed passenger/cargo ship. The passengers had limited deck space available. However, there were only twenty-two passengers in all.

---

[56] The church, located in the Canal Zone, was a part of the Methodist Episcopal Church in the U.S., not the mission conference in Panama.

# Building for the New

> Ports of call:
> September 27, 1957, Cristobal, Panama
> September 28, 1957, Buenaventura, Colombia
> October 2, 1957, Callao, Peru
> October 5, 1957, Arica Chile
> October 6, 1957, Antofagasta, Chile

We were traveling together with the Pace family, Jim and Evelyn and little Jimmy. Because of the size of our family, we had two cabins. Because we had small children, we were scheduled to eat before the others. Our destination was Antofagasta, Chile. The voyage took over three weeks mainly due to the many stops in ports along the way to discharge cargo. In the evening, some form of entertainment was offered. We played bingo or a horseracing game. Sometimes we had a movie. When in a port, there were no evening activities as the crew was occupied with unloading or loading cargo. In several ports, the ship did not dock but unloaded into lighter or small boats. We watch in several ports with a degree of anxiety as cars were swung over the side to be dropped into a lighter. Mary and John celebrated their birthdays while on board the ship. One of John's favorite snacks was butter patties.

Finally, the day arrived when we entered the harbor of Antofagasta.[57] The ship docked, and we headed to the hotel which we were instructed to use. We were told the weekly train to Bolivia had left the day before we arrived. We were now faced with a six-day wait until it went again. After almost a month on a ship, we were now faced with how to entertain three children for six days in a hotel. The truth is, they seemed to enjoy it. The hotel staff gave them special attention. During the day we investigated the city, especially the parks. And for a diversion, we took one bus line after the other and rode to the end of line, and then rode back. We got to know Antofagasta that way.

---

[57] Antofagasta was originally a part of Bolivia. It was a part of the Departmento del Litoral. It also became known as *The Pearl of the North* because of the wealth from mining that passed through the port. Bolivia lost this department to Chile in *La Guerra del Litoral* (the War of the Seacoast). Basically, the war was over the rich minerals in the area. The treaty allows Bolivia special port rights in both Arica and Antofagasta.

Excitement built when the day arrived for us to board the train[58] to Bolivia on October 13 for an overnight trip. It had been a while since missionaries had traveled to Bolivia by ship. As a result, we had the dubious honor of conveying eighty-six items for missionary families we carried as hand luggage. Because of all our luggage, we booked two staterooms. The trip was over twenty hours, departing in the evening. It turned out that I occupied a stateroom with all of the hand luggage, while Rachel and the three children slept in another. It was some time in the early morning hours, there was a knock on my door. It was the Bolivian customs officer beginning to get some of his work done as we crossed the border. Fortunately, the year in language school helped. However, I was sure he had seen other passengers, more experienced travelers to Bolivia, who paid part of their customs charges in liquid form.

Shortly after we crossed the border into Bolivia, we were joined by Le Grand B. Smith who had ridden the train down from Oruro to welcome us and bring us the news that while it had been proposed we would be assigned to the American Institute in La Paz, we were to change trains in Oruro[59] and go with him to Cochabamba where we would be appointed to serve Central Methodist (Spanish) and Union Church (English) and teach at the American Institute in Cochabamba. Actually, I felt a degree of relief. I was not trained to be a teacher. Because I spoke English did not mean I could teach it. My career was planned to be a local church pastor. Mr. Smith explained we were to live, for the time being, in a vacant villa owned by the American Institute next to the campus. I was to begin serving

---

[58] The Ferrocarril de Antofagasta a Bolivia (The railroad from Antofagasta to Bolivia) was the result of a concession by Bolivia to Melbourne Clarke & Co. Construction began in 1872. By 1882, the railroad reached Oruro, Bolivia. In 1888, shares were floated on the London stock market. Subsequent routes were added in Bolivia from there. The train reaches the highest point in a pass in the Andes at over 15,700 feet.

[59] Oruro, located in the Andes at over 10,000 ft. above sea level, was settled by the Spanish as early as 1606. Oruro is the rail junction for the mines and for the cities of the interior. Built on a sacred site for the Uru people, it is the folklore center of Bolivia. Its annual ten-day carnival festival is inaugurated with a procession of persons dressed in colorfully embroidered costumes and masks which is followed during the ten days by a struggle with the Devil (Diablada).

as pastor of the Union Church immediately. The rest of my proposed assignment as outlined would be confirmed at conference a month away.

It was a cool October day when we climbed off the train in Cochabamba. This was to be our home in the country, not of birth but of choice.

Cochabamba is nestled in a beautiful green valley at about eight thousand feet above sea level. It is known as *the city of eternal spring* or the *Garden City*. The valley was evidently inhabited by indigenous groups for thousands of years. The valley, unlike the Altiplano, is Quechua-speaking. It was part of the Inca Empire. The Inca used the method of relocating people into a conquered area, and thousands were said to have been resettled as a means of pacification of hostile populations. It was also said that the Inca used the valley for the production of maize that could not be grown on much of the colder, higher lands of the empire. The first Spanish to inhabit the valley was Garci Ruiz de Orellana in 1542. It is said a registry indicates the land was purchased from local tribes in 1552. The valley acquired its name in 1786 when the city was named *Cochabamba*. The change in name was done to commend the city for the pivotal role it played in the suppression of an indigenous rebellion of 1781.

In 1812, Cochabamba was the site of a rebellion against the Spanish army. On May 27, thousands of women took up arms against the Spanish. Nathaniel Aguirre, a historian, indicated, being outnumbered, the men withdrew from the encounter, but the women of the city stood fast against a force of five thousand Spaniards. Their bravery was a battle cry through the remaining battles for independence. General Belgrano gave incentive to his men with the cry, "Are the women of Cochabamba present?" A monument stands on a small crest in Cochabamba to honor those heroic women. A reminder of their bravery is the celebration of Mother's Day in Bolivia observed on May 27.

## Queque-Queque – Our Frist Home in Bolivia

We were taken to the American Institute in Queru-Queru. The long lane sloping uphill to the school was lined by tall eucalyptus trees. It was an impressive sight.

We were guided to Los Chorillos, a large old estate separated from the school by an adobe wall at least six feet high. The old mansion was on an uphill slope, U-shaped, with a fountain situated in a flowerbed in the middle. The property was not exactly rundown but it was rustic. We were to share this with a Russian couple who were acting as caretakers. They spoke minimal Spanish and no English. Ed and Natalie Barber lived in the missionary residence to the right just inside the grounds. Slightly beyond stood the impressive high school building of the American Institute. On the third floor was an additional missionary residence occupied by Cecil and Mary Tinder. Up the hill were the rest of the classroom buildings for the primary level. The director's residence was a lovely cottage situated among trees. There was another adobe wall behind the primary building and the director's home beyond which was another large section of property belonging to the school for future development.

What was then known as Central Church, which stands a few blocks from Cochabamba's main plaza, is a lovely stone chapel. It is here the Spanish congregation and the English church met for services. The church building, as so many of the properties at that time, was relatively new. I was asked to assume responsibilities at the Union Church immediately because of the heavy load the missionaries were carrying at the school.

Villa Chorrillos was very old and poorly furnished. One thing we had to be on the lookout for were vinchucas.[60] The ceilings of the rooms were not plastered but canvas that had been nailed up and painted enough over the years that they had become a hard surface. But the vinchucas lived in the attic area. They came down at night. To protect the children from being bitten, they slept under mosquito nets and with the legs of their beds in cans filled with kerosene. We made do and enjoyed the camping-style of living until it came time for the Annual Conference. The conference was to be held here in the school in Cochabamba in November. It was only about a month from the time we arrived, which passed very rapidly.

---

[60] More popularly known as the *kissing bug* because of its desire to move around the mouth. It also can infect anywhere because it leaves feces on the skin which, when scratched, causes an infection that can be fatal. It is common in Argentina, Brazil, Bolivia, and Chile.

Murray Dickson was responsible for organizing the conference. Bishop Barbieri arrived from Buenos Aires to conduct the conference. As must have been in the early conferences on the frontier in the U.S., the gathering of church workers, missionary and national, was like the homecoming of a great family. Many of these had not seen one another since the meeting of the last conference.

# Chapter III

# The Bolivia Annual Conference 1957

The Annual Conference was held in the American Institute in Queru-Queru. The pastors and delegates were housed in the dormitories used for boys and girls. There was a great deal of excitement; some had not seen each other since the last Annual Conference. Then there were several of us who were recent arrivals not known to all of the other missionaries nor the delegates. Bishop Barbieri was on hand to chair the sessions. He resided in the house for the director of the school. Ed Barber had been filling in because the Kents were in the US on health leave.

The national pastors, church delegates, and missionaries were still experiencing the afterglow of the fiftieth anniversary celebration the year before, and of the fiftieth anniversary celebration of the American Institute of La Paz earlier in the current year. It was reported to the conference that the American Institute was decorated by the president of the republic, five cabinet ministers, and six ambassadors—the previous president, Hernan Siles Zuazo, was a graduate of the school, two members of the cabinet, the minister of Foreign Affairs, the Minister of Finance, and the current ambassador to the United States. The report went on to indicate that "one of every eight Bolivians listed in Who's Who in Latin America studied at one of the Methodist schools."[61]

---

[61] Murray Dickson Report to the Board of Missions, December 22, 1957

This was my second meeting with Bishop Barbieri. The first and only time to date was back in Garrett Seminary in 1954. The events of the week went well. The conference was like a big family reunion. We soon discovered that to the children, all the adult missionaries were *aunt* or *uncle*. It was all one family. The big moment was the conclusion of the conference with the reading of the appointments and the serving of communion. My appointment was to Central Church and Union Church, Cochabamba. Anibal Guzman, a recent graduate of the seminary in Buenos Aires, was pastor since 1955. Anibal was well-liked by the congregation. He had been able to attract many of the students from the American Institute to activities at the church. Anibal was the first full-time pastor the church had. His pastoral style built up the congregation.

The McCleary Family in front of the Central Church

Parsonage (El Salvador), Cochabamba. Rachel is holding Mark Paul, Leslie Ann, Rachel Mary, and John Wesley.

The church was a lovely stone building that would have passed for an English countryside chapel constructed in 1947. It sets on the corner of Mayor Rocha and Baptista. The entire property is enclosed with an attractive stonewall about six feet tall, with the upper part being slatted wood allowing a view of the street. There was a two-story classroom building on the front of the property close to the street. It had been the primary school building of the American Institute and now served as a kindergarten run by the church. Behind the school building was a large playing area with a volleyball court.

We moved into an almost new parsonage situated on the back of the lot behind Central Church. The parsonage was the nicest house we had lived in; a two-story building with three bedrooms upstairs. It was of recent construction, having been built in 1955. It was a spacious house with a study immediately inside the front door, a large parlor, and dining room across the entire width of the house. In addition, the downstairs included the kitchen and a guest bathroom.

We soon became acquainted with Don Crispín and Dona Rafita. They were the caretakers of the property and lived in a small hut built into the far corner of the lot, affording them a view of the entire property. We learned that Dona Rafita cooked over an open fire outside of the hut. John, just two years old, found that to be interesting, and was fed samples of the cooking by Dona Rafita.

The Sunday schedule was a full one. The services began at 10:00 a.m., with a service in English for the Union Church. Bolivia had granted oil concessions to several US oil companies, and the operations for the companies were located in Cochabamba. By the second year they had been relocated to Santa Cruz. During the service in English, the Spanish Sunday school met in the classrooms of the kindergarten building. At 11:00 a.m. was the service in Spanish. Both services, we discovered, were well-attended.

The congregation of Central Methodist Church was my primary responsibility. At the time, the church had less than fifty members but always ran well over 100 at morning worship. It was a difficult decision to join a Protestant church. For some, being a Catholic was not as much a religious experience as it was cultural or national identity. Also, family ties are close. The membership consisted of teachers and former teachers of the American Institute; professional people, some of whom were graduates; merchants; and persons who had come to Bolivia as refugees from Europe.

And faithful attendees were the families of missionaries. It would be a very unusual Sunday not to see Nova Dickson in the congregation. It was definitely a middle-class congregation. Another was the Franz Frank family. Franz was Swiss and ran a construction supply company. Another faithful family was a German couple who ran a store. They had spent the war in a relocation camp in North Dakota making pine crates to ship lend-lease to our Allies. During the war, the CIA had a long reach. Periodically, there would be someone from the Jewish community in the congregation. Their children were in the American Institute. They seemed to be more inclined to attend a Protestant church rather than the Catholic. There was no synagogue in Bolivia. The rabbi in Santiago, Chile, would ask to come and use our church for special festivals of the Jewish calendar about twice a year.

One of the activities of Central Church was a kindergarten. It ran during the week on the calendar of the American Institute. The Institute accepted children who had attended our kindergarten. We had space for just less than one hundred. There were always more applicants than we could accommodate. The teachers we had were all just exceptional women. There was one; I wish I could remember her name. She had such a way with those little bundles of energy whose parents understood parenting to mean letting the child have his way.

My responsibilities included teaching a class on religion to seniors in the high school. Because of Anibal Guzman's good work, there were a number of youths from the American Institute high school who attended Central Church. Anibal had also started a mission at kilometer 0 on the road to Santa Cruz in 1955. By 1956, the congregation raised enough money to buy a property at that location. A small brick building had been built which was used on Sunday afternoons to have a Sunday school for small children. A kindergarten was started here by Rosa Shelielian, a missionary from Argentina.

The country was in the straits of serious inflation. The price of tin had drastically dropped. The demand also had decreased. A smelter in Texas that smelt Bolivian ore was closed. News only got worse. The State Department and Bolivia had agreed to a stabilization plan that went into effect in December 1956. It called for a floating exchange rate. Bolivia was a food dependent country, with imports running as high as almost 80 percent of foodstuffs. Prices rose rapidly, while wages were frozen. Juan Lechin initially supported the stabilization plan, then switched to oppose it in line with the miners' condition. It wasn't just tin but other metals mined in Bolivia—tungsten, zinc, and lead. The foreign exchange loss was playing havoc on the economy. As part of the stabilization plan, the U.S. subsidized 30 percent of the national budget. Exchange rate fell from sixty bolivianos to twelve thousand between 1952 and 1956. During our first year in Bolivia, the exchange rate was fourteen thousand bolivianos to one US dollar. The largest bill Bolivia had in circulation was ten thousand bolivianos worth less than one US dollar. Everyone, and I mean literally everyone, had a bank account in the U.S. in dollars. All imported goods disappeared from the shelves of stores. To offset the conditions, the State Department did not offer hard currency but food aid. This, too, had adverse consequences for the economy. It was easier and cheaper as well as better tasting, for example, to get the US flour than flour milled in Bolivia. Another product in large tins readily available in the market was cheddar cheese. The Bolivians did not have a taste for cheddar cheese and preferred to sell it for what they could get than eat it.

In 1958 the International Tin Council to stabilize the market, cut Bolivia's quota of 33 percent. Setting in motion layoffs mandated by the International Monetary Fund to keep costs in running the mines in line with income. By September 1958, the International Tin Council abandoned prices supports. One who knew well and loved Bolivia was US Ambassador Philip Bonsal. On being reassigned to Cuba in early 1959, he was supposed to have stated in his last report to Washington that in spite of all the aid from Washington, Bolivia was worse off than in 1956.

In spite of conditions in the country, in a matter of months, the church work had grown. In the neighborhood known as Tupuraya, another mission was started. It was begun near the home of the Franz Frank family by members of Central Church. Franz's two children were students at the American Institute and members of Central Church. The daughter, a high school student, with others of her class, started to gather a group of small children on Sunday afternoons. The youth of the church were willing to assist with extension work. About twenty youth would gather at the church Sunday afternoons around 2:00 p.m. The group would divide into four smaller groups and head out on bicycles. One group would go to kilometer 0, another would go to Tupuraya, and the others to two sections of the city. Each group gathered the neighborhood children on a vacant lot to play games and share Bible stories. A snack made from US powdered milk and bread made from US flour were given the children. By 4:30 p.m. the youth returned to the church for the MYF meeting. Two of the first two locations soon grew into preaching places (avanzadas), and then churches Bethel and El Nazareno (The Nazarene).

At 7:30 p.m. was the third service of the day for working class persons for whom Spanish was not their first language. There was no bulletin for this service. The service was less formal. More hymns were sung. The hymns were lined out. A line would be sung and then repeated by the congregation. There was always a contest for the one who could repeat from memory the scripture from the week before. Non-readers depend much more on memorization. Usually there were several who remembered it. Different persons lead in prayer. The sermon was most frequently from the parables or miracles of Jesus. It was stories they could remember and retell. It was never a large group, usually fifty or less. For me, it was a meaningful way to end Sunday.

One of the families from the Tupuraya neighborhood walked into town to attend the Sunday evening service. I tried to find them to call on them. That part of town was just a squatters' settlement with no street names or numbers. I finally located the family. It was a small square building made of adobe blocks and a tin roof. The wife was already beginning dinner over an open fire. She insisted I come into the house. It was a low doorway for even my 5'2" height. There were no windows. A table with tin utensils sat in one corner. A pile of mats was stacked in the other corner. Near the door was a backless bench, so I sat down. It took a moment for my eyes to adjust to the semi-dark. She insisted I have something to eat. Her concern for hospitality was greater than her poverty. I repeatedly I did not care for anything. She insisted and went to the table and picked up an aluminum wash basin with three eggs in it. She proceeded to crack and peel the shell from one. She had been cooking over an open fire. Her hands were not clean. There was no running water in the house. By the time she finished peeling the egg the white had changed color. She approached and offered it to me. I hesitated. She glanced down and realized the reason for my hesitancy and popped the egg into her mouth to clean it, and offered it to me. What quickly ran through my mind was to measure what my rejection of the egg would mean to her and what the consequences might be if I accepted it. A missionary is confronted in many situations where he must decide if he is willing to pay the price and identify with the poor.

I remember well March 3–5, 1959. Riots broke out across Bolivia as an anti-American protest. What triggered this flash point was a story in *Time* magazine that an unnamed source in the US Embassy said that Bolivia and its problems should be divided up among its neighbors. Rioting broke out for several days in cities across Bolivia. US government property destroyed $70,000.

I had several errands to do. I drove a green Studebaker pickup truck at the time. The children saw I was opening the gate to get the truck out and asked to go along. I signaled for them to climb in the back of the pickup, and we left. I went over a block so that as we came up to the plaza I would be on the right side of the street for the post office. A block over, I turned the corner to the right and a half a block away was a huge unruly crowd in front of the US Information Service building. There were people throwing canisters of films and movie projectors out of the second-floor windows. I turned to the left instead, slowing enough to be able to shout to the kids to lay down and sped off for home. I pulled into the property and shut the gates. I called to Crispin to close the front gates and to put a ladder up against the adobe wall behind the house in case a rapid exit was needed via the neighboring property. I asked Rachel to turn on the news and to fill the bath tub with water and to close all of the blinds. That evening the family slept on the floor downstairs. I slept upstairs where I could keep an eye open to see if anyone was climbing the walls. The morning news told of rioting across the country, of buildings broken into and defaced, and of vehicles in motor pools burned. A quick survey of the church and two-story classroom building indicated that not a single window had been broken.

During our first year, Bishop Barbieri contacted me to indicate that he was sending a young man to come work with me. I was delighted with the news. It meant that not only would I have some help with the church work but it would mean there would be someone close with whom I could have some companionship. It was something I would never regret. Bishop

Barbieri had met in Rome a young priest who had reached the decision to become a Methodist. Jose Carlos Diaz arrived soon after. Jose Carlos, a priest from Spain, was studying in Rome. The process of his studies had arrived at the decision he could not accept the infallibility of the Pope. Having arrived at that conclusion, he could no longer be a Catholic. Jose Carlos was an intelligent, gifted companion. I enjoyed his enthusiasm and positive outlook. In a year, we were given another appointment in Santa Cruz, but Jose Carlos soon was also given an assignment near us in Montero at the Wesley Seminary and the Rural Institute.

Our church custodian, Don Crispin, was a neighborhood fixture. Both he and Dona Rafita were Quechua-speakers and illiterate. Crispin was a veteran of the Chaco War.

He was not Methodist and did not attend any of the services but would slide in the side doorway to the church throughout the service to listen. In the evening, he would take a stool and open the front gate of the church to sit on the corner to watch the traffic. He was a humble person and was always warmly greeted by passersby though he would not speak first. Bishop Barbieri encouraged that church buildings be named from biblical sources rather than locations. One of the events during the first year was to have a contest to choose a biblical or religious name to replace the name *Central Church* for the church. It was no surprise when the committee reviewing the suggestions found one that said, "The Church of Don Crispin." The committee, however, finally agreed on a name meaningful to their experience, *El Salvador* (The Savior).

The two churches of which I was pastor required quite different services. As could have been noted, El Salvador Church was focused on evangelistic outreach. My responsibilities for the Union Church were similar to those of a chaplaincy: one of offering pastoral care to a well-defined group of people who had special needs. At the time, the Bolivian government saw oil as a substitute source of income to replace mining. Oil concessions were granted to North American and one European companies.[62] There were two types of employees of these companies: the office managerial staff

---

[62] The matter of concessions and the importance of oil to Bolivia will be dealt when our move to Santa Cruz is presented.

and the oil riggers who worked on the concession, drilling test wells. As quickly as operations started, the offices would be moved to Santa Cruz to be closer to the concessions. Hardly any of them spoke Spanish. They felt alienated from the community. The Americans had a basic fear of what might happen. The wives, whose household responsibilities was taken over by maids, looked for outlets for their time. They socialized together which might include spending playing cards and drinking. For most of them, the church played a heightened role for them. The two, so different congregations for one pastor, produced an almost unresolvable tension. The national political climate was of major concern among the members of the Union Church.

One of the evident signs that appeared with more frequency was a simple one, "Yankee, go home!" For women whose husbands were out on an oil concession three of every four weeks meant they spent considerable time alone. One of the most obvious places of such a message was on the wall surrounding the airport. However, some thoughtful person with a different attitude had added underneath, making it now read, "Yankee, go home! And take me with you!"

During our second year in Bolivia, political tensions continued. Accusations against Americans grew. Nearing Christmas, one of the Americans employed in a program related to Point Four Program hosted a small farewell party in his home for a group of about fifty American friends, Bolivian fellow workers from the office, and other Bolivians. The man's family had already left the country to be home for Christmas. The husband was to leave at the end of the year. I attended the party having had the family in the English-speaking services of Union Church. About 9:00 p.m. a disturbance broke out in the living room among two or three men over what records would be played. The host, American who was soon to leave the country and for whom the farewell was being given, stepped into the struggle going on and was killed by a knife stab. Rumors flew as to why he was in Bolivia and whether this was to settle a score before he left. As one can imagine, the incident heightened the anxiety among the Americans. The incident was never publicly addressed.

In Cochabamba there were other things happening in addition to those attached to Central Church and Union Church. A small congregation was budding in the American Institute in Queru-Queru. Ed Barber was shepherding this flock. When the agreement was made in 1924 that the Canadian Baptists would provide religious services in Spanish, the congregation that had existed was no longer related to the Methodists. The Methodist missionaries, who ran the schools, however, were determined to hold their own services. There began in the American Institutes in both La Paz and Cochabamba services in the schools. In the case of both schools, there were boarding sections with live-in students. These children were not required but encouraged to attend along with the missionaries. A church had been started by Bill and Martha Kent who had come to teach at the school in 1950. Wilson Boots, in addition to his teaching assignments, was pastor in 1954. Wilson and I had met at Garrett Seminary when we started our first quarter there in 1952. It is a small world.

An additional new ministry in Cochabamba was the Paul Harris Home for Crippled Children. The Rotary Club had taken a special interest in crippled children. It was an unmet need which seemed to be growing. Under Rotary Club sponsorship, a home for crippled children was created. The Rotary purchased a property and furnished it with basic equipment and furnishings. It sought an organization willing and capable of carrying out a program for handicapped boys and girls. Franz Frank, a member of El Salvador Church and president of the club, approached L.B. Smith about assuming responsibility for its operation. The appropriate discussions took place with the conference and with the Rotary Club, leading to a contractual agreement for its operation.

In 1960, the home began operations under Methodist auspices, with the presentation of the keys to the house by Dr. Serafin Ferreira to L.B. Smith. Teresa Silvera, a missionary from Uruguay and a teacher trained in phytotherapy, was assigned to the home.

There occurred a special event in the McCleary family during the second year of their assignment. A fourth child was born into the family on May 4, 1959. We decided to give him the names of two New Testament missionaries, Mark Paul. Mark was a premature baby born in the clinic we had come to use for the family. Bolivia was one of the few countries where the board had policy of a midterm break of two months in the four-year term. We decided that July and August would be the best time for the break, and that the requirement of going to sea level could be met just as cheaply to go home as going to the coast. Besides, but both sets of grandparents were dying to see Mark Paul.

During these first two years in Bolivia, I had an opportunity to understand better the operation of the Bolivian church. Bishop Barbieri was a respected and revered leader. His plethora of responsibilities permitted him time to visit Bolivia only twice a year. He was heavily dependent for the day-to-day operations of management of the church in Bolivia on Murray Dickson. Murray carried the title of executive secretary, which meant he did anything the bishop asked of him. Murray was a faithful, loyal support to the bishop. He was a doer. Murray was a visionary with the ability to make things happen. I am sure the bishop recognized this and was the reason Murray had the job. Both he and the bishop shared the same vision for Bolivian Methodism. They shared a kinship in that regard.

It was interesting to sit back and watch Murray operate. Murray knew how to influence the right people and find money when he needed. He saw to it that influential people got an invitation to visit Bolivia. One delegation we hosted was composed of a chief justice of the Texas Supreme Court, the president of Houston-Tillotson College, Austin Texas, the conference president of Methodist Men for the Southwest Texas Conference, and a prominent rancher from the valley. He tracked Southwest Texas clergy like Don Redmon who was appointed to the Board of Missions Education and Cultivation Department. He also knew that while this was needed for growth, the maturity of the church would come when it was Bolivian. The Lands of Decision program was smothering the Bolivian church with North American personnel and money. Both the bishop and Murray recognized this.

Barbieri directed personnel from his other conferences to Bolivia. Among the first was Theresa Silvera, Rosa Sheleileon, Pablo and Marta Monti, Dr. Chiccatti, and Rev. Guicheney. Barbieri was invited by the Council of Brazilian Bishops to speak at a conference. In return, he asked them to designate a visitor to go to Bolivia for a two-week visit of all of the projects and to speak at the Annual Conference. He was shrewd. Barbieri contacted the Kyodan (United Church of Japan) to send a missionary pastor to the Okinawan colony in Eastern Bolivia. Their reply stated they would be honored to provide a missionary to Bolivia. Bishop Barbieri was one of the presidents of the World Council of Churches based in Geneva. While in Switzerland, he touched the Methodist Church of Switzerland for funds for a project in the Beni of Bolivia.

I read some of Murray's correspondence for the year of 1958. He wrote the head of the seminary in Brazil for a scholarship for a student from Bolivia. He was asked, did he have someone to send? He replied no, he just wanted some place ready when the next candidate came along. Rev. Okada, chairman of the committee on Overseas Evangelism of the Kyodan Church, appointed a Rev. Makino as missionary to Bolivia. It turned out Mrs. Makino was in very poor health that did not permit them to come. Murray did not let the Kyodan off the hook. He followed up on Bishop Barbieri's contacts to get a substitute to be interviewed by Bishop Barbieri in July when he was in attendance at the World Sunday School Conference. Both Barbieri and Murray knew how to cut the bureaucracy to do things. They were both operators. Barbieri did admit it existed. He just didn't see it. Murray knew it was real and existed, but he also knew how to work around it. Together, they made a real pair.

The Board of Evangelism, in cooperation, sent teams of Methodist pastors as evangelists to preach in conferences in Latin America. They were always good preachers. They came to the El Salvador Church while I was pastor there. They needed interpreters. Five languages were spoken in Methodist churches in Bolivia on any given Sunday. Murray wrote to the Board of Evangelism to indicate that there were ten evangelists in Argentina who wanted to come on preaching missions to Bolivia. Why was he writing the Board of Evangelism? Was Murray writing to ask if the funds for the travel of the US preachers could be used for the travel of the ten from Argentina? And he added a twist of the arm, saying the air fares will be considerably cheaper.

Incidentally, who was the bishop in Argentina who selected the team? It was Bishop Barbieri. A second letter went to James Ellis, the area secretary for Latin America of the Board of Missions. Murray noted he knew there was a travel fund at the area secretary's discretion. Could he make available funds for the cost of travel inside of Bolivia for ten pastors from Argentina coming for two weeks? What were they doing? Because of the predominance of the North American presence, they were working to be sure that Bolivian Methodism was fully integrated into Latin American environment.

There was another step toward autonomy they both supported. One of the instruments that would need to be in place along with Conferencia de Iglesia Evangelicas Metodistas en America Latina (CIEMAL) was a Latin American Board of Missions. Murray was named a member of the Board of Missions of CIEMAL.

# Chapter IV

## Annual Conference 1959

The Annual Conference met in the fall of 1959 in Cochabamba. Our numbers continued to grow. The work was expanding into new forms, as well as new areas geographically. Murray Dickson was again responsible for the preparation for the conference. Bishop Barbieri represented the Latin America Central Conference. Buenos Aires was the episcopal area to which he was assigned.

The conference closed with my appointment to start a new church in Santa Cruz and to be superintendent of the Eastern District. We were due to take a midterm leave of two months. We could not see it as being too comfortable to go to the coast somewhere in Chile for two months. We decided to fly home to Illinois. Both sets of grandparents liked the idea of seeing the grandchildren, so we left for the States. In preparation for the trip, we explained to the three we would be flying to Miami and be met by my parents. Once they knew about the trip, they could hardly stop talking about it. We were constantly being asked, "How many more days until we go to your Ami?"

It meant arriving to an Illinois weather after the lovely weather of Cochabamba. I rented a car in Miami to drive to Illinois. The cheapest car rental I could find was a local agency. The first day drive north from Miami, we discovered the car did not have a heater! Rather than losing time by turning around and renting another car, we stopped and purchased blankets. But once in Illinois, we parked the rented car and used family cars!

It was delightful to see relatives on both sides of the family. We stayed with grandparents on one side of the family, and the second month with the other. They lived close enough together that we could see both sets of grandparents on almost a daily basis. We were kept so on the go, we could hardly consider it restful. But the change was definitely refreshing to the soul. And the familiar home cooking was good for the body.

When we returned to Bolivia, we returned to Santa Cruz. Our responsibilities were to replace Bob and Carmen Gnegy until they returned from the States. One of their children had had an eye accident when she was hit by a piece of colonial roofing tile. The surgery and recovery would take months. So we occupied the house the Gnegys' rented. Bob and Carmen were a special couple. Bob was gifted in his ability to work among the poor. Carmen was from Puerto Rico, fluent in Spanish, and a wonder with women. The work in Santa Cruz was based on early exploration by a visit from Rev. Corwin Hartzell. However, it was not until 1952 when a serious attempt was made to start a congregation.

> Lazareto was an appropriate name for the neighborhood. In the Bible, Lazarus was the one Jesus raised from the dead. In the tropics, there are numerous diseases, such as leprosy and tuberculosis, for which the sick was isolated from the well. The cemetery was most frequently located on the cheapest land which was outside of the city. Those with an uncurable disease were expected to live in isolation outside of the city. In this case, when the city was started four hundred years ago, they went to Lazareto—the village of the living dead.

In 1953, L. B. Smith was named district superintendent of the Central District, pastor of Central Church in Cochabamba, and pastor of the congregation in Santa Cruz over five hundred kilometers away! Their Santa Cruz work was built on by persons who had graduated from both the La Paz and Cochabamba Institutes. At conference the next year, Javier Ormachea and Glady were assigned to Santa Cruz to carry on what the Smiths had started. The Gnegys had purchased property and relocated the congregation to the Lazareto neighborhood, a suburban of Santa Cruz where they had begun an extensive program for children and women. A vital congregation was developing in Lazareto. This was a community that had grown next to the cemetery and, at that time, was at the edge of town.

Santa Cruz was about to experience phenomenal growth. A road encircled the town (circumvalacion). The cemetery was outside the road, but the property with the small open chapel was just inside. The Gnegy family lived in what had been the main house of a large hacienda. However, it needs to be explained that the government had expropriated the land in the Land Reform. The house we occupied was surrounded by a military camp since the land had been expropriated. From 10:00 p.m. at night until dawn, armed guards were posted at the gate to the property. We felt completely safe at night.

Other Methodist workers frequently would come to visit Santa Cruz on vacation because of the climate and to get out of the elevation. On one such occasion, Bill Frank, a missionary teacher assigned to the American Institute in Cochabamba, came for a few days' visit. His flight, unfortunately, arrived after the guard had been placed at the gate to the farm house area. Flight schedules were uncertain. It was a considerable loss of time to wait for a flight to arrive. Since I wasn't sure when he would be coming, we waited up for him. We heard a taxi jeep pull up to the gate. All vehicles in Santa Cruz at the time were jeeps. The Indian raw conscript stationed at the gate halted the jeep and ask who was wanting in. A voice answered in Spanish with an American accent, "Teniente Frank!" And came the reply, "Pase, senior!" (Advance, sir!) From then on, Bill was known as *Lieutenant Frank*.

There was another visitor from Cochabamba who came to spend some time with us. Ligia was a teacher at the American Institute. She probably did not realize it, but her companionship with Rachel was very helpful at the time.

We had a somewhat unusual visitor from the board. Dr. Eugene Smith sent a message that he would like to spend a few days with us. His visit was after we had moved for the third time in Santa Cruz into the larger of the two houses on the new property purchased for the Alfa y Omega congregation. We had met Gene when we were processed as new missionaries. When he arrived, it was obvious he needed time away from the office. He actually spent little time with us. It was a special gift to have his presence with us for four days.

Living in the middle of an army base, during the day, we had young men walking up to ask for help in washing their clothes, for a snack of food, or just come by to visit with someone. During the day, we had young men walking up to ask for help in washing clothes, for a snack of food, or just come by to visit with someone. It was something like six months before the Gnegys returned.

Also, Bob and Carmen loved pets which they kept for their three daughters. The pets included four horses, a parrot, and a monkey, whose chain was connected to the wire clothesline. It does need to be said that our four children enjoyed the animals. I must confess I did too. There was no mail delivery. We had to go to the post office downtown every day for our mail. The streets weren't paved. The sandy streets allowed the runoff of the tropical downpours. The sidewalks were three to four feet above the street. Also, there was a city ordinance that one could not ride a horse into the streets that formed the four sides of the main square.

I rode horseback downtown most every day for the mail and anything else that needed to be done. The horse was to be tied to a hitching post on a side street off the main square. It was then a walk of a block or so, to the post office up and down the elevated sidewalks to the bank, shops, restaurant, or ice cream parlor.

On one of my morning trips to the post office, I had just removed our mail from the box when a man approached me. I had noticed him standing by the door when I came in. He was holding an envelope in his hand. He explained his son had been conscripted for the army. It was over two months since his son had left home. This was the first letter he had received from him. He was anxious for the news. He remarked he had forgotten his glasses at home and asked would I read it to him. I replied that I would be most happy to read it to him. I read the pencil-written, scrawled note. I folded it and placed it back in the envelope for him. He thanked me profusely. By his dress and his demeanor, I was sure it was not a matter of his forgetting his glasses. With a son in the military who could not pay his way out of the annual conscription, the father, like so many others, was, in all probability, illiterate. And the son, two months before he wrote? Maybe the son himself was just learning to write since he was in the service. In Bolivia, the two-year conscription was one of the ways young men were integrated into the social order. There was no doubt in my mind he represented the masses of Bolivia's poor and powerless.

> The Department of Santa Cruz is the largest of nine departments or counties in Bolivia. In land area, it is about one-third of the country or a little smaller than Montana. It comprises the eastern third of the country sharing borders on the north and east with Brazil and with Paraguay on the south.
>
> The Department of Santa Cruz is the heart of the farmland in Bolivia. The agricultural products raised are sugar, cotton, soybeans, and rice. Governments since the revolution of '52 have placed a priority on the use of modern farming techniques in the Santa Cruz area where weather allows for two crops a year. Petroleum and natural gas discoveries are also significant export items producing foreign exchange income. A nationwide referendum in July 2004 approved a regulated exportation of the natural gas.
>
> The composition of the population would be approximately:
> Mestizos 57%
> Natives (Chiquitano, Chane, Ayoreo, resettled Quechua and Aymara) 30%
> Caucasian (European, Canadian, United States) 12%
> Asian (Okinawan, Japanese, Korean, Pacific Islanders) 1%
>
> The city of Santa Cruz was first founded in 1561 by Spanish explorer Ñuflo de Chavez about 200 km (124 mi) east of its current location, and was moved several times until in the late sixteenth century. For much of its history, Santa Cruz was mostly a small outpost town even up until the Revolution of '52. The agrarian reform had a high priority on agriculture and internal migration which caused the city to grow at a very fast pace. The city is one of Bolivia's most populous. It "produces nearly 35% of Bolivia's gross domestic product, and receives over 40% of all foreign direct investment in the country." This has helped make Santa Cruz the most important business center in Bolivia.

The year was passing rapidly. I had spent considerable time on the work of the district. Imagine being named district superintendent of a new district with two churches! But several things had happened.

My first responsibility now that I had to keep the work in Lazareto going until the Gnegys got back was to buy a downtown property and start a church. This is the second time I thought back to seminary. My first time was in Costa Rica when I wondered why I hadn't been taught more about street preaching. Now I was wondering how I missed learning what one does to start a new church.

It wasn't difficult to start church services in English. Many of the Americans had been part of the Union Church congregation in Cochabamba before moving here. A cooperative school in English had been started for the children. The oil men were field hands who worked on the oil rigs. Their shifts were three weeks on the oil rig, one week at home in town. Several of the American families were Methodist and supported our Spanish work.

The other congregation, a Spanish congregation, soon to be given the name *Alfa y Omega*, had to be formed in a quite different manner. Groundwork for the new church was prepared by others. This was destined to be an urban congregation. It was in the fastest growing city in Bolivia, fifth fastest in the world and second fastest in Latin America. It was small now, and it was backward. However, it would become second or third largest city in Bolivia in the center of the agricultural heartland and oil fields of Bolivia. An additional congregation formed quickly to fill that need. It was an honor to be sent to this most dynamic part of Bolivia in terms of economic growth and political change.

L. B. Smith had paid an early visit to Santa Cruz to identify former students in La Paz and Cochabamba. Javier and Gladys Ormachea built on L. B.'s visit. When I began my ministry, it was natural to first look up persons who had attended or graduated from one of our Methodist schools in La Paz or Cochabamba. My predecessors left a list of persons who had had some contact with Methodism. This brought together a nucleus of persons. Other pastors sent me names of their former members who had moved to Santa Cruz. I looked around for civic clubs or places where persons with a more national or global outlook might gather. I found two.

One was a business association of store and business owners who were beginning to think about a different kind of city. It was the beginning of a chamber of commerce. The other was a group of men who were stamp collectors. Several of these men were of foreign descent. Both groupings were people who had outside contacts and communications. This was to be an urban congregation, not one growing out of running a school or clinic. It would take time. It would require a lot of contact building.

Top row: John, Rachel Mary, Leslie Ann
Mark Paul, being held by Sawako, and Paul McCleary
1959, Santa Cruz

Another dimension to starting a church was identifying a location. Were there other Protestant churches in Santa Cruz? Where? There always seemed to be *church drifters*—persons who went from congregation, looking for something and then moving on.

There was another Protestant church. It was known as Rev. Ackerley's church. It was a faith mission begun by a single individual with a conservative theological position. One day, Rev. Ackerley came to see me to become acquainted. I was glad he took the initiative to come. I looked forward to establishing a cooperative relationship. He first wanted to know my position on the story of Jonah being swallowed by the whale. I am afraid he did not appreciate my interpretation of the Bible story. He left abruptly, and our friendship never developed.

When the Gnegys returned, I was able to rent a house within two blocks of the plaza to be able to study out the city's flow and life. In the city center, all buildings were built up to the sidewalk and in a solid block. The house we occupied was deep, with rooms around two courtyards. The rooms around the first courtyard were the rooms for more family quarters—the living room, dining room, bedrooms, and bath. The rooms around the second courtyard were the service rooms, the kitchen, laundry, maid's quarters, storeroom, second bathroom. This was not intended to be a residence of long occupancy. It was going to be a base of operation until a property could be determined for the site of the church and parsonage.

Montero was just beginning to blossom. It was at the end of the highway that opened in 1955, and linked Montero with Cochabamba and the rest of the country. Bob and Rosa Caufield arrived in 1955 and began planning and building the rural institute. Eventually it would be an elementary and vocational high school. The demonstration farm grew with the school. Bob was exceptional at developing a vocational school and farm out of raw jungle. The school widened its curriculum with Harry and Pat Peacock (1960), Wendell and Ruth Kramer (1960), and Judy Good (1964). The vocational school joined the new approach to a post-revolutionary nation. It was in harmony with the five steps in the MNR agenda for Bolivian education.

The Paces arrived at the same time we did in 1957. Jim and Evelyn were a part of the Montero enclave. Jim was given the task of starting a seminary for training Bolivian leadership for the church. For seminary training, new candidates for the ministry were being sent to the Facultad Teologica (Union Seminary) in Buenos Aires. The seminary was an excellent one, but it was too far from the realities of Bolivia. Jim's theological training at Yale Seminary and his keen sense of social justice gave him the right mix to training a new ministry for Methodism in Bolivia. A second son was born to the Pace family on February 11, 1958. A heavy blanket of grief covered the Methodist family in Montero and across the country as news spread of the accidental death of little Richard Steven on May 6, 1959.

An important addition to this complex in Montero was the dimension of public health. Dr. Jim Alley and Jean arrived in 1964. Jim brought a completely new perspective to the Methodist medical program in Bolivia. Frank Beck arrived in Bolivia in 1912 as a teacher for the American Institute in La Paz. He became convinced what was needed was a doctor. He returned to the U.S. to undertake training for a new vocation. Dr. Beck set a high standard for all who followed him. The American Clinic and School of Nursing in Obrajes and the clinic in Ancoraimes resulted from his change in vocations. These institutions set a standard of good medical practice and quality patient care that made them outstanding in health delivery in Bolivia. There followed him Dr. Bill Jack and Mary Lee Marshall (1956) who guided the medical work with great compassion and skill for many years. Dr. Pablo and Marta Monti and Monica (1956) served in the hospital in La Paz, and then in the program in in Santa Cruz. Dr. Lou and Sidney Tatum (1960) arrived soon after we did. Lou was a gifted surgeon who left us too soon but left us with fond memories of his warmth and gentleness. Dr. Enrique Cicchattii (1960) was assigned to the Altiplano, trained both as a minister and doctor. Dr. Toby and Marjorie Thompson (1963) were a good addition to the medical team at the hospital. Dr. Jim, the first public health doctor who was assigned to Montero, and Jean Alley (1964). Dr. Lindsay and Ann Smith (1967) were added to the staff at the hospital where Dr. Lindsay soon became director.

Just as so much of the Methodist work in Montero was of a new kind, so too was the medical practice. Jim began his medical practice by taking a public health survey of Montero. The survey covered items such as did the house have running water, inside toilet, what kind of floors? How many children in the family? What is the frequency of pregnancy and what of the health of the mother, of the child? What vaccinations did the family have? And what food does the family eat? Eggs? Meat? Milk? Jim had a good profile of the condition of families in a frontier town. And Jim smoked. When his assignment to Bolivia came to the missionary committee in Bolivia, his smoking took up a lot of discussion. I think why the members of the committee finally accepted his coming was that they wanted to meet a public health doctor who smoked. That seemed like a real contradiction. Jim attracted young intellectual persons such as Jim Becht and Henry Perry to provide the person-power to the jobs done. Other students of Bolivia from missionary community were Lesli Hoey and Marshall Martin, to identify a few.

Montero was the end of the highway that connected Eastern Bolivia with Cochabamba and the rest of Bolivia. However, it was only the beginning of a vast rural area being carved out of the jungle. There were several colonies already started when Bob Caufield first began to clear the land for the rural institute. It was a group from Canada of European descent.

The very first colony of settlers to move into the Chaco was in 1927. It was a small group of persons called *Russian* Mennonites. Originally from Russia, this body of conservative Mennonites had settled first in western Canada but, disaffected due to the requirement for obligatory military service during the World War I, moved again, some to Mexico but others to the Chaco. The disposition of the Chaco War found them in Paraguay.

In 1930 and 1947, the Paraguayan Mennonite colony was augmented by more Mennonites directly from Russia. In 1954 and 1957, a first group of thirty-seven families from various Mennonite colonies in Paraguay established Tres Palmas colony, twenty-five kilometers northeast of Santa Cruz de la Sierra.

In 1963, new settlements were founded by Mennonites from Paraguay and Canada. In 1967, Mennonites from Mexico and Belize settled in the Santa Cruz Department. *Las Piedras* colony was founded in 1968 exclusively by Mennonites from Canada. Most settlers in Bolivia were traditional Mennonites who wanted to separate themselves more from *the world*. Altogether, there were about seventeen thousand five hundred Mennonites living in sixteen colonies in Bolivia by 1986.

A few months before the passage of the Agrarian Reform Law in October 1952, the Ministry of Agriculture approved a planning for colonization by an organization known as Uruma Society. It had been organized in 1950. President of the Uruma Society was a man named Jose Akamine, a longtime resident of a northern town known as Riberalta. He and a small number of persons of Japanese descent came to South America as railroad workers in Peru. As time passed, he crossed into Bolivia to work in the rubber industry. Aware of conditions in Japan at the end of the war, he wanted to offer to others the same vocational path he had taken almost fifty years earlier. At the time the Uruma Society petition was presented, it already owned over fifty thousand hectares in Santa Cruz, with a model family farm operating on it with seventy-three hectares of cotton and corn under cultivation. Four houses have been built with fifteen Japanese in occupancy. The Uruma Society plan contemplated bringing three thousand Japanese or Okinawan families over the next decade.

The reality, however, was that the vast majority of the Okinawans came under a plan of the US Department of State. The sovereignty of Okinawa passed from Japan to the United States with the signing of the peace treaty ending World War II. As part pf the defense perimeter in the Asia-Pacific theater, the US military occupied 45 percent of the arable land for air bases. The displaced farmers were offered relocation in Latin America in either Brazil or Bolivia.

The oldest colony of Bolivians was the Yapacani, a colony created to make a grant of land to a veteran of the Chaco War. It was begun about the time of the signing of the peace treaty in 1938. Unlike the other colonies already discussed, the colonists were hardly given more than a parcel of land on which to live. Their existence depended on a continuing connection with the extended family in the highlands.

It was essential to add staff to the base in Montero to meet the expanding and growing needs of the settlers. One of the first to be added was a couple from Japan to relate to the Japanese colony, San Juan, and the Okinawan colonies. The correspondence files indicated that by 1958, Murry Dickson and Bishop Barbieri were close to coming to a determination with staff of the Kyodan (United Church in Japan) for a clergy to serve in Bolivia. Communications sent to Dickson and Barbieri indicated that the candidate who had been selected failed to pass the health test for final approval. A new candidate was being put forward for consideration by Bishop Barbieri. An interview was arranged for Bishop Barbieri during his attendance at an International Sunday Conference in Tokyo in July 1958 to meet the candidate. After the interview, Bishop Barbieri and Dickson sent their concurrence to the Kyodan. Rev. Katsumi and Yoshie Yamahata arrived in Bolivia in 1959. A new parsonage was built for the Yamahatas with special attention to what would be common to a Japanese home. Katsumi had worked on a US airbase following WWII. As district superintendent, on any given Sunday morning, there were five languages spoken in the eastern district of the Methodist Church.

Another source of staff was the Mennonite Central Committee (MCC).

In 1955, Frank Weins, on leave from MCC Paraguay, visited Bolivia wearing his hat with the resettlement office of Point Four Program, a recently inaugurated international aid program of the US government. There were two Mennonite colonies in Bolivia. One at Tres Palmas settled in 1954, and the second settled in 1957 were Mennonites from Canada. There was no in fractural support and both were in extreme poverty. The Methodist missionaries in Montero had encountered similar conditions in colonies near them. The conditions required from extension teams to work in the colonies. They had also determined that such deployment had to begin work on the level of the people. What was needed were young men who could farm at a non-mechanized level of farming. The easiest solution would be to ask the Methodist Board of Missions for such personnel. However, there would be the matter of adjusting to less than modern conditions. Information had reached the Montero staff that the Mennonite colonies had signed an agreement in 1959 for young men to work in Bolivia as a form of alternate service to the military obligatory draft. Men coming would be under an MCC program called PAZ, the Latin word for peace. In addition, the Methodist program would qualify for MCC volunteers, which means women would also participate in the program. By 1964 when a country director was appointed by MCC there were nine volunteer and PAZ men in Bolivia—three were working in the Mennonite colony, Tres Palmas, two were assigned to the Southern Cross Radio Station in La Paz (Canadian Baptist), and there were four assigned to the Methodist, and two were added by the end of 1960 to Rural Institute in Montero. Lori Wise, archivist at the MCC in Akron, PA, indicated that across the years, a total of seventy-three volunteers and PAX men had been assigned to the Methodists.

Periodically, as district superintendent, I would visit one of the colonies for a quarterly conference or some other responsibility. I remember well one of my visits to the congregation that had developed in the Aroma colony. I was there for an evening service. The building was both church and parsonage in the same building. It was a long hut with tin roof with the *sanctuary* at one end and a one-room parsonage at the other. We were in the midst of a service when we began to hear a noise which was constant and increasingly louder. It was obvious we should suspend the service to deal with whatever was occurring. The men present immediately went outside and began filling a very small trench around the hut with kerosene. I was told we were about to experience a migration of army ants. began to at an appropriate moment, they lit the kerosene and kept it burning. For several minutes we were in complete isolation from the rest of the world. Gradually, the sound grew softer as the ants moved on past us. I was told that as the land was cleared and the jungle cut back, this was a less frequent experience.

Anibal Guzman was the district superintendent for the Central District. Anibal was on scholarship for a year for studies in Buenos Aires. I was asked to include the Central District in my responsibilities for the coming year.

For the 1960 conference, the place and date had been set as Cochabamba, December 27 through January 1, 1961. With the much large number of missionaries, especially with children, it was suggested that other arrangements be made for them. The four McCleary children were left in the care of Sawako, a woman from the Okinawan colony who lived with us as a member of the family assisting Rachel with the household chores and a companion to the children. As the conference was concluding, word reached us that Mark Paul had drowned. Due to the poor municipal water system in Santa Cruz, rainwater was collected in a ground level cistern. Sawako was planning to do some wash and removed the cover when someone came to the front door. In her absence, evidently, the child wanted to play in the water and fell in.

Gulf Oil flew us to Santa Cruz on their plane. We were confronted by not our grief alone but the concern for Sawako, who wanted to take her own life because of what she thought was her failure. We called on Katsumi for assistance in consoling her. The next day, Murray arrived and insisted that we move out of the house where the accident had occurred. In a daze, we relocated to the only place available on such short notice which was a property rented for oil families. Some Cruzeño had that idea of building a motel in a style he had seen in the U.S. which was a series of small separate cottages, which were basically one very large room a small kitchenette and bath. When Gulf Oil relocated, they rented the entire set of cottages. We were able to sub-rent from Gulf. It was a make-do move but accomplished what seemed best at the time. It just added pressure to my task of locating suitable property.

I had spotted an ideal location. It was a few blocks from the main plaza in a residential area. It was owned by a man who was planning to relocate out of the country. The property was a corner lot with a facing on both streets. Next to each side of the lot was a house. The one house with garage was occupied by the owner of the property. In the interim before a church could be built on the corner lot was adequate for a parsonage with the large living room and dining room for the chapel. The other home was smaller in size of more recent construction of brick. His asking price was more than I thought it was worth, but he was willing to consider a counteroffer. The final price we agreed on was $22,000, which, in today's dollars and market, even in Bolivia, was a steal. The owner wanted to be paid in dollars and in cash.

Murray flew from La Paz to Santa Cruz on December 22, 1960, to close the deal. The owner had been anxious for the sale. He quickly vacated the property so we could move in. In the large room that was almost half of the house the owner had a grand piano. It was something he wanted to sell and was ideal for the sanctuary. Memorial gifts flooded from friends in Bolivia and families in the U.S. With the gifts, I ordered a carpenter shop to made pews for the sanctuary, a pulpit, and pulpit chairs. A hallway starting at the front door split the house in half—to the left was the sanctuary; to the right, the rooms we used for our family. A bathroom and kitchen were at the far end of the house and an enclosed porch we used as a living room/dining room. The garage was finished off so it made an excellent study. It was quite adequate as parsonage and chapel.

An assessment of the changing situation of religion in Bolivia suggested several changes had developed. The Roman Catholic Church was the dominant religious entity, but not a monolithic one in spite of its claims. The outsider who had any contact with the Catholic Church came to recognize that there was an institutional framework that was rigid and out of step with the changes brought by the 1952 revolution. There were also elements in the church that were more liberal and with which outsiders could find some resonance. Regarding Protestants, there was a narrow middle ground made up of the Methodists and Canadian Baptists and a few ecumenical or cooperation agencies. However, there was a growing number of conservative evangelical churches and church agencies beginning to enter the country primarily since the revolution. These would be represented by entities such as the World Gospel Mission and the Wycliffe Bible Translators.

The reason for such a narrow middle group among the religious community was due to the instrumentality put into place about 1905 by the mainline churches. It was the cooperative agreement known as the comity agreement which governed the missionary expansion of the mainline Protestant churches. Its purpose was to avoid duplication and conflict among Protestant churches. Several of the church-related agencies created to assist with aspects of human development came to Bolivia. One of these already referred to is sponsored by the Mennonite Central Committee known as PAX—a program of alternative service for those who due to religious convictions will not bear arms.

Another is Heifer International. While PAX provides manpower, Heifer International provides livestock. It came into existence in 1944. It is a faith-based non-governmental agency whose program developed in response to the devastation in Europe during World War II. Heifer International was started by an Ohio famer who was a member of the Church of the Brethren, one of the peace churches in the U.S. During the Spanish Civil War, West had volunteered as a relief worker. His involvement caused him to work alongside Quakers and Mennonites.

In 1938, one of the projects they worked on was a program to feed hungry children. Later, reflecting on his experience of feeding children, he wrote, "These children don't need a cup [of milk], they need a cow." When he returned home, the thought continued to haunt him about the best way to feed hungry children. He shared his thoughts at church and with his neighbors.

In 1939, an entity was formed: the Heifers for Relief Committee. By 1944, the committee had been incorporated with recognition as a public charity. It made its first shipment to Puerto Rico which included seventeen heifers—donations from farmers of a similar persuasion as West.

As knowledge and experience grew, it was natural to consider ways in which the program could embrace the reproductive aspects of a livestock program. At first, West asked farmers to donate pregnant heifers who would produce a calf. Heifer International also took the next step of including other livestock such as goats, sheep, chickens, pigs, fish, bees, frogs, and rabbits.

It was an ideal entity to invite to join the work of the rural institute and the extension program into the several colonies. The first ship to Bolivia was to Santa Cruz for delivery to the rural institute in Montero. A cargo plane from Florida was bringing a shipment of eighty-six goats, two or three pairs of rabbits, and two young bulls. The plane got to Chile but was running into bad weather to cross the cordillera of the Andes.

For three days it made an effort to make its way through passes to get to Santa Cruz. It was entirely off schedule. Every day I went to the airport to inquire if they had an ETA (estimated time of arrival) for the flight. By this delay, news of the flight spread by word of mouth. It was news that spread that the Methodists were bringing in a planeload of livestock. Many people in Bolivia in 1961 had little opportunity to fly; they could not imagine persons who transported animals by plane.

On the fourth day when I arrived at the airport the flight had already landed. The plane was sitting near the runway a short distance from the airport building. They had the freight door wide open with a cattle gate across it wide a large fan to cool the plane. Imagine, the livestock had been on the plane for three days. They were now in the tropics with the temperature at around one hundred degrees. As rapidly as I could, I notified Montero that the plane had arrived. Then I put into motion the plans we had made for trucks to transport the livestock to Montero over an hour away. A makeshift chute was pushed up to the open freight door of the plane, and the goats were rapidly loaded into trucks. The rabbits were and they too were not hard to unload. However, the young bulls were not happy campers. They were restless from the heat and from being penned up for so long.

The plane was on a slant. The plane had not been cleaned for three days. The bulls had been penned up near the pilots' cabin. It was a matter of someone working his way up the slope of the plane, then opening the gate wide enough for the bulls to get out and clear their route of exit. Since I represented the party contracting the planeload, I was designated to be the one to open the pen for the bulls to exit. The floor was so slippery I had to work my way forward hand over hand by gripping the side of the body of the plane. It was not difficult to let the wood frame, serving as a gate to block the bulls, simply swing back. I made my way as quickly as I could back to the freight door on the side of the plane, grabbed the doorframe, and swung myself up and over the cattle chute on to the ground.

As I picked myself up off the ground, I turned as I was startled to see that the bulls were not in the truck waiting for them but had followed me and jumped the chute! The bulls were enjoying their freedom, running freely on the land strip of the airport. We called around the airport to some of the farmers who had horses. They then tried to corner the bulls who had no intention of being cornered. The airport tower alerted all incoming flights, and over half an hour passed before the bulls could be loaded on a truck. It was an episode I did not wish to remember, but I believe I was told both died prematurely from heat exhaustion. Nor will I make any remarks about the goats who ate all sorts of plants on the semi-cleared jungle pasture in Montero. Several other shipments arrived from Florida.

There was a postscript to the arrival of the animals. That is that the two men piloting the plane had to spend almost a week in Santa Cruz until a new motor could arrive from Florida to replace the one burned out in crossing the Andes. Both the pilot and copilot had been in one branch or the other of the service in WWII. Due to the lack of good streets or roads in Santa Cruz, all of the taxis were old jeeps. There was little entertainment for the two men, and they had little interest in visiting church projects. On more than one day, they had frequented a bar before lunch. Inevitably, I would receive a call about *my* two pilots. On one such morning, they had commandeered a taxi and were enjoying reliving WWII by exploring the town. I could not measure the amount of damage that the total experience cost the reputation of the Methodist Church. No one doubted, however, the amount of publicity and interest we received from it. Our learning experience from the first shipment was enough to make all of future shipments easy work.

Another instrumentality formed by churches was to respond to combat illiteracy soon emerged in Bolivia. Frank Laubach was from the town of Benton, Pennsylvania. He graduated from Princeton University (1909), received a theological degree from Union Theological Seminary, New York (1913), and a doctorate (PhD) from Columbia University (1915).

In 1912, Frank and Effa Emaline, a nurse, were married. On completion of his doctorate in 191–, the couple sailed to the Philippines as missionaries of the American Board of Commissioners for Foreign Missions (ABCFM). The Laubachs were involved in evangelistic work among the Muslims.

In 1921, he was appointed to the faculty of Union Theological Seminary in Manila. In his evangelistic work, he was serving mainly among illiterate peoples.

As he struggled to reach the highly resistant Moros, he found that the system he had developed for learning Maranao could be adapted to teach people to read their own language. Enthusiastic reception of the program led to rapid expansion, and when American mission support for literacy teachers dried up with the onset of the Depression, a local chief ordered each learner to teach others. The *Each One Teach One* principle, together with graphic charts linking pictures with words and syllables and wide distribution of simple reading materials for new readers, constituted the Laubach method.

In 1935, Laubach began to introduce his method in other countries, and in 1945 he was appointed *missionary at large* of the ABCFM to work with Lit-Lit (the Committee on Literacy and Christian Literature) of the National Council of Churches in the USA. which he had helped establish. After he retired in 1945, Laubach formed Laubach Literacy Inc. to work worldwide, and in 1968 he launched Laubach Literacy Action to work in the United States. His work touched 103 countries, involved 313 languages.

In Latin America and the Caribbean, it was known as ALFALIT. ALFALIT was one of the most widely embraced programs from the international community. ALFALIT was started by Eulalia Cook who sought out the collaboration of two Cuban educators, Justo Gonzalez, and his wife, Dr. Luisa Garcia Gonzalez, to assist her with her literacy program. Eulalia found the Laubach method to be the most successful she had tested in teaching an illiterate individual to read and write within a few months.

The office for ALFALIT was based in San Jose, Costa Rica. It first gained wide acceptance in South America, and then spread to the Caribbean and the United States. Later, another literacy program created by Paulo Freire, a Brazilian educator. became very popular in Latin America. Bolivian Methodists adaptive the program with enthusiasm. While Heifer International was a program rural in nature, it fit well into what Methodists wished to accomplish in the new settlement areas of the Alto Beni, Chapare, and Santa Cruz. The ALFALIT program was important because it could apply to both urban and rural settings.

## Cooperative Partners and Competitive Gospels

There have been other church entities evangelizing in Bolivia almost as long as the Methodists have been here. The most established Baptist church has been the Canadian Baptist with which the Methodists have had a long-standing posture of cooperation. One of the most helpful studies I have seen is the doctoral thesis of Wilson Boots in which he draws a comparison among the Methodist, Canadian Baptist, and the Bolivia Indian Mission.[63]

The comity agreement signed by mainline churches for many years was an obstacle for traditional Protestant churches to begin work in Bolivia. Faith missions or Pentecostal churches do not accept such agreements. Where there is a form of cooperation, it is due to the disposition of the individual and is not an organization guideline.

---

[63] See *Protestant Christianity in Bolivia: Mission Theory and Practice in Three Mission Churches* by Wilson Boots, The American University, 1971.

The Seventh-Day Adventists began about 1915; this was about the time Bishop Oldham organized the Bolivia Mission Conference. They began work among the Aymara around Lake Titicaca. The Bolivian Indian Mission began work among the Quechua about the same time. It has gone through mergers and is now the Union Cristiana Evangelica. Other churches working in Bolivia are the Oregon Friends that began on the Altiplano and spread to the Yungas. The Assemblies of God entered Bolivia probably about the time of the revolution. The Church of the Nazarene, World Wide Mission, as well as other Pentecostal churches have established missions.[64] Some of these missions claim the truth and position themselves as over against others to define a space for themselves.

These are parachurch organizations with whom the Methodists have a cooperative agreement or understanding. Several of these have been referred to already—Heifer International (agriculture, livestock), ALFALIT (literacy program), LAOS (short-term technical volunteers of diverse skills), Mennonite Central Committee (agricultural, medical technicians), and Wycliffe (Bible texts, translations, linguistic training). These parachurch relationships provide services and ministries that need not be duplicated. They are noncompetitive relationships which can prove to be of value at any time in the future.

---

[64] Information about missions in Bolivia may be found in *Latin American Church Growth* by Read, Monterroso, and Johnson.

# Chapter V

## The Annual Conference 1961

The Annual Conference for 1962 was held in January 1962. Less than three weeks before it was to meet, tragedy struck the Methodist Church again. Murray Dickson and Dr. Lou Tatum were traveling to Caranavi in the North Yungas. It is noted as being one of the most dangerous roads in the world. It is mostly designated for traffic to move in one direction until noon, and then in the opposite for the other half of daylight. Evidently, they were forced from the road by a truck hauling lumber. The vehicle fell several hundred feet.

Murray and Nova arrived in Cochabamba in April 1943. Their three children—Francis, Margaret, and George—were all born in Bolivia. Murray and Nova taught at the American Institute for several years, and then Murray served at acting director and director for several more years. He served as director of the school in La Paz for the year 1957. He also served as pastor of the Union Church of El Salvador for several years. He served as district superintendent of Central District for four years. Murray was serving as district superintendent of the Northern District when he was traveling to Caranavi to hold a fourth quarterly conference at the time of his death. He was also serving as executive secretary of the annual conference since 1958. Murray's name was added to a list on a monument in Cochabamba dedicated to honoring outstanding Cochabamban teachers. His name was the only foreigner, the only Protestant, and the only representative of a private school.

Dr. Louis Tatum III and Sidney, along with their two daughters, Nancy and Sarah, arrived in Bolivia in February 1960. Lou was a gifted surgeon who came to Bolivia to cover for Bill Jack Marshall at the Pfeiffer Hospital in Obrajes, while the Marshalls were on furlough. In a very short time he came to be recognized for his skill as a surgeon and for a caring, outgoing personality. Hearing the news that Dr. Enrique Cicchitti was ill, Lou decided to accompany Murray to the Yungas.

Bishop Barbieri arrived in La Paz from Buenos Aires the day after the tragic accident. I flew to La Paz to receive the bishop. When his plane touched down and came to a full stop, I walked out on the tarmac to receive him. I was waiting for him to deplane at the bottom of the steps. Silently, we shook hands. His first words were, "Where is your family?" Aware we were due for furlough in the U.S., I told him they had left two days ago. Then we stopped walking, and he looked me hard in the eye and said, "I want you to be executive secretary of the conference." I was not prepared to hear that. My mind was struggling with the significance of that assignment.

We drove down from El Alto into the city in relative silent. Our next stop was to visit the grieving families. I had gone to visit Nova the day before soon after my arrival from Santa Cruz. Nova was standing in the front yard, which I thought was a little strange. She told me that we could not go inside now. There were two men there from the US Embassy going through Murray's study. We remained in the yard and conversed until they left.

After our visit with Nova, I took the bishop to see Sidney. A young widow, Sidney was rightfully angry and grieving at the loss of her husband. The bishop's stay was brief. In two days, Barbieri returned to Buenos Aires.

With the Annual Conference less than three weeks away, it meant picking up the pieces on the planning for the sessions. The days passed rapidly. Somehow, the conference occurred without any problems. It is hard to explain what it means to lose two very significant members of a small tightly knit community bonded together by their faith and commitment to serving others in a foreign country. We went through the motions fulfilling our responsibilities as an organization. We comprehended our reality. Our community had lost two individuals, but now we were going to lose the wives and children of those two men who were our friends and colleagues. Our loss was heavy. All of the small Methodist community felt the grief.

The last day of the conference opened with the traditional reading of the appointments and the service of communion. Jim Pace was named district superinfect of the Northern District and executive secretary of the Annual Conference. He would need to move to La Paz.

The next day I boarded a plane to join Rachel and the children who had spent Christmas and New Year's with her parents and mine. It would be such a joy to be with all of them again.

# Chapter VI

## January–October 1962

### The Family Furlough in the United States

For missionaries, a term of service in Bolivia was usually four years on the field and one year at home. The home leave was to fulfill several purposes. We renewed family ties. We visit our supporting churches. We educated congregations about the context in which we lived and worked. Our children wore native costumes, and we presented slide shows. More importantly, we informed congregations about the Board of Missions policies and programs we were implementing and expanding in Bolivia. We also shared our faith through storytelling and preaching. Home leave also gave us the opportunity to acquire training and skills for the next term on the field.

Finally, the majority of Bolivia is located geographically in high altitudes in the Andean mountains. For years, Methodist work in Bolivia was from eight thousand feet elevation to over twelve thousand feet elevation. The Board of Missions medical team considered staying in the high altitude for a prolonged period of time a health risk. Missionaries voluntarily could opt to return home after four years, as well as take a midterm leave of two months to vacation at sea level.

In discussions with the board, it was evident they had been advised that Jim Pace would assume the position of executive secretary, but that I would return from furlough to take up that work. I was to visit the churches that had only recently assumed an interest in the work in Bolivia to establish a continuance of support. In addition, it was important to visit those congregations supporting my past and current work. I was presented an itinerary that included my home conference and the sixty churches of the Bloomington that contributed half our support, along with other churches of the Central Illinois Conference; the Southwest Texas Conference, especially St. Luke's United Methodist Church in Houston and First UMC; and Lover's Lane churches in Dallas. In addition, there was a group of thirteen churches from the northern suburbs of Dallas known as the Fertile Crescent; the pastors of which I met. Also, there were churches in Oklahoma, especially Boston Avenue in Tulsa. These contacts were for promotion of the total work in Bolivia. As it turned out, I visited and spoke at two hundred churches or district gatherings and three seminaries in 285 days.

For some of the visits to churches in Illinois, I involved the family. These contacts were of a different nature and more for the support of the family. One of the things that helped communicate the diversity of indigenous groups in Bolivia was our daughters' modeling native dress with the distinctive regional style of hat. It is the custom in Bolivia that each tribe be identified by the hat style that the women wear. The Quechua wore a stovepipe hat they whitewashed every year. The Aymara wore Borsellino-style bowler hats. Women expressed individuality by the color. I was told the ribbon and knot in the cord around the crown of the hat conveyed whether they were single or married. Our daughters attracted the audience's attention and allowed me to introduce the complexity of communicating across cultural lines with diverse religious beliefs and practices.

During our furlough in the summer of 1962, I requested the opportunity to be participate in training that would help in transcultural communications and understanding.

It was a National Training Laboratories Institute for Applied Behavioral Science, known as the NTL Institute. The NTL Labs is a program in the field of behavioral psychology. Founded by Kurt Lewin in 1947, it occupied a facility in Bethel, Maine. The leader of the six-week seminar I attended was Warren Benne, successor to Lewin. In the group of over one hundred attendees, there was one other minister, a Lutheran pastor. The rest were from corporations seeking ways to improve the management skills of headquarters' staff. Most of the time we participated in *T* groups structured along psychological lines. Rachel was not included in the program. She was with our children on her family's farm in Illinois. I called her almost every night to share with her what we had talked about or done. I did not want this experience to develop a gap between us.

In 1947, Kurt Lewin founded NTL Institute. It is a training program in behavioral psychology. The method of teaching programs for corporate training Lewin and others developed is called the T-groups model. Lewin died early on in the project but continued under the leadership of cofounders Ron Lippitt, Lee Bradford, and Ken Benne, among others. Ken Benne was with us the entire time. The NTL Institute exerted a significant influence in the human relations movement in post-World War II management thought.

I was looking for something that would be useful as a form of intercultural understanding. There was no doubt that if I would be assigned to a managerial post it would require skills in communication and understanding cross-culturally.

The date of the Annual Conference in Bolivia was moved back to October. To attend the conference meant that the furlough would be ten months long. In addition to speaking engagements, travel and correspondence took up significant blocks of time. I had not been able to give as much time to what I would be doing back in Bolivia or how the church situation might have chances in the months I was away. I wondered if I had put off too much thinking about it because I really hoped that Jim Pace would find himself so inspired that he would continue as executive secretary. But I was sure of one thing, that the institutional development of the church was changing and needed to be moved along the road to new stages of development.

One of the events of major significance was the election of John F. Kennedy, president of the United States, which had occurred just before our furlough began. It was our good fortune to be in the States during his time in office.

John Fitzgerald Kennedy (JFK) was elected the thirty-fifth president of the United States who served from 1961 until his assassination in December

1963. He was the youngest president the U.S. had had to date. At the time of his election, his administration brought a wave of euphoria across America for the freshness and youth it brought.

Kennedy was really a part of the aristocracy in America—born May 29, 1917, into the prominent Kennedy family of Brookline Massachusetts and son of the distinguished Joseph P. Kennedy and Rose Fitzgerald Kennedy. The father was a businessman and politician. His mother was a socialite and philanthropist. His paternal grandfather was a Massachusetts state legislator. JFK's maternal grandfather had served two terms as mayor of Boston and in the US Congress. He was hardly plebian stock. All four of his grandparents were Irish immigrants who did well. JFK was the second child of nine children.

Although a Catholic, JFK graduated from Harvard University—the most outstanding Protestant university in the U.S. During World War II, he distinguished himself commanding PT Boats in the Pacific theater of the war, earning both navy and marine corps medals for heroism. JFK ran for a seat in the US House of Representatives from Boston from 1947 to 1953. He decided to run for a seat in the senate and won to become the junior senator from Massachusetts from 1953 to 1960. JFK published a book, *Profiles in Courage,* in 1960 which was awarded a Pulitzer Prize. JFK narrowly won the election against Richard Nixon. His campaign did not take off until after the televised debate with Nixon, which was the first such event of its kind. He was the first Catholic president of the United States.

Kennedy came into office with a load of heavy involvements to deal with. The president was under pressure to increase US involvement, while university campuses boiled over with anti-war sentiment. The large issue of the Cold War was an unsolvable issue which brought headaches to the presidency from the Middle East as well as Central America and Cuba. He increased the number of US advisors in Vietnam and initiated the strategic hamlet program. By April, he was turning attention to the Western Hemisphere. He authorized an attempt to overthrow the Castro regime in Cuba with the faulted Bay of Pigs invasion in April 1961. US spy planes discovered the Soviets building a missile base in Cuba in October 1962, taking us to the brink of war with Russia over the Cuban missile crisis. The resolution of the missile crisis did not resolve the tension which erupted again in the Che Guevara incident in Bolivia to be dealt with later.

Two major accomplishments of the Kennedy administration were of great importance to Bolivia, and they were the Alliance for Progress plan and the establishment of the Peace Corps. Both came early in JFK's short administration. JFK also made an attempt to diminish the impact of racism and support civil rights through a new program called New Frontiers. During furlough, I traveled constantly to almost all parts of the U.S. The Kennedy administration was being well received in most parts of the country. In Texas where the northeast was not appreciated, having Lynden B. Johnson as vice president brought positive degrees of respect to administration. Kennedy was assassinated on a visit to Dallas, Texas, on November 22, 1963.

His death was far out of proportion to the event itself. In Catholic Latin America, the significance of a Catholic as president in United States was an immediate cause for exuberance. The youthfulness Kennedy and his administration reflected was a close second in importance to his religion. The Alliance for Progress and the Peace Corps was perceived as positive interest in Latin America. These aspects of the new administration in Washington was a reversal to widely held public opinion concerning the intent of the U.S.

Following my mission work in Bolivia, I served as executive director of Church World Service of the National Council of Churches in the USA. One of the minor responsibilities was to maintain an active relationship between it and the Ecumenical Council in Cuba to avoid what had happened with Protestantism in China when the country became communist. Quarterly, I flew to Cuba to meet with church leaders (Methodist, Presbyterian, Anglican/Episcopalian, Baptist) and to preach in churches. It evolved to include the release of American prisoners from prison in Cuba and an aid program in Cambodia, among other things. On almost every trip I was taken by a representative of the council to visit the member of the Central Committee of the Party who had the portfolio of Education and Medicine (which also meant religious institutions). On at least four occasions, this also included a visit with Fidel Castro. Our conversation began at around 9:00 or 10:00 p.m. and concluded about 2:00 a.m. Fidel was knowledgeable, informed, and an interested learner. We only met in offices of the party's international section. We did not exchange gifts. At least one member of the Ecumenical Council was present. I always took U.S. citizens with me to clarify, if need be, any misinterpretation of the visit. Since the charter plane could carry five passengers, there was not an extra charge. They were from education or business, and only once did I include a member of Congress, Eleanor Holmes Norton; persons such as John Sagan, treasurer of Ford Motor International; James Laney, president of Emory University (later U.S. ambassador to South Korea); and Jim Wall, editor of the Christian Century. Also, a doctor was included in the team as frequently as possible who could help me understand the health condition of those with whom we met.

# Chapter VII

## Germany's Multi-Presence

The German influence in Bolivia should not be ignored. One of the three tin barons was a German who greatly influenced the tin market as well as that of other minerals. The only national airlines was operated by Germans. German pharmaceuticals dominated the market in Bolivia for many years. Loans and financial services were, for a time, dominated by Germans. The German predominance over the Bolivian military extended from the training of officers in Germany to commanding Bolivian forces during the Chaco War. What was at play during our years in Bolivia was the US manipulation of a strategy to displace the influence of Germany in Bolivia.

There were three waves of German-speaking immigrants to Bolivia. The first came as early as the 1920s. It was Mennonite immigrants from Russia via Canada and some via Paraguay to take up land in Eastern Bolivia. Much larger waves of Mennonites arrived in the '60s and '70s. The process of migration was made much easier due to the support from the Mennonite Central Committee in Akron, Pennsylvania. The number of German Mennonites in Bolivia was sixty thousand by 2010.

The second wave of Germans began in the late 1930s. This group was essentially Jewish refugees from Europe who were helped to resettle in Bolivia by Maurice Hochschild, the tin baron. He secured a special agreement from President German Busch Becerra, who was of German descent, for visas of European Jews to resettle in Bolivia. Hochschild helped found the Sociedad de Proteccion a los Immigrantes Israelitas and founded the Sociedad Colonizadora de Bolivia. Reference has already been made to the contacts and assistance the Methodist Church offered the Jewish community. They settled in urban centers, primarily La Paz and Cochabamba. There were German schools in Oruro, Sucre, Cochabamba, and La Paz. The Jewish population has declined due to emigration to Argentina, United States, and Israel.

> Notable German Bolivians
>
> - *Ronald Rivero Kuhn*, footballer
> - *Hugo Banzer*, military officer, twice president
> - *Germán Busch*, military officer and president
> - *Luciano Durán Böger*, writer and poet
> - *Enrique Hertzog*, physician and President
> - *Pato Hoffmann*, actor and theater director
> - *Noel Kempff*, biologist and environmentalist
> - *Jaime Mirtenbaum Zenamon*, classical guitarist and composer
> - *Alberto Natusch*, military officer and dictator
> - *Erwin Sánchez Freking*, footballer
> - *Achim von Kries*, German military officer
> - *Blanca Wiethüchter*, writer and poet
> - *Jorge Wilstermann*, aviator
> - *Lidia Gueiler Tejada*, politician (the first female president of Bolivia and the second woman in the Americas to ever become chief of state).
> - *Luis Gamarra Mayser* singer and songwriter, (from Waves of Migration Wikipedia)

The third wave were former Nazis and fascists also fleeing Europe who frequently moved to Bolivia from Argentina or Uruguay. Prior to WWI, Germany replaced France as the major market for Bolivian exports. By the 1930s, the three tin barons were more at home in Europe than in Bolivia. General Hans Kundt led the Bolivian military throughout the Chaco War and maintained a relationship with the Bolivian military for over twenty-five years. It was stated, "Bolivia was, in short, a classic semicolonial country totally beholden to competing imperial power for finance and technology." The military coup of 1936 brought into power two colonels, David Toro and German Busch. In 1937, German Busch unseated Toro to become the solo head of state.

The two major US unions, A.F.L and C.I.O., and State Department sent the Magruder Commission to Bolivia to investigate the Catavi massacre of on December 20–21, 1942, when hundreds of miners and their families were machine-gunned in a labor strike as Penaranda's administration spun out of control. In April 1943, Vice President Henry Wallace visited Bolivia to consolidate US–Bolivian relations. The Patiño mines established their corporate headquarters in Delaware, giving it the status of an American corporation. On December 4, 1943, Bolivia declared war on the Axis powers. By December 20, the pendulum swung back. The Penaranda government was replaced by a military coup led by Major Gualberto Villaroel. The new government was immediately recognized by Peron in Argentina. This was Paz's first government position as member of the Villaroel cabinet which was made up of four military officers and three MNR members.

It was at this time that Murray and Nova Dickson were acclimating themselves to Bolivia.

The Villaroel government suffered a continual sequence of national strikes. It attempted to initiate plans for rural schools and a rural labor code. In May 1945, it organized a conference of indigenous peoples with one thousand five hundred in attendance. This experience was a basic training experience for the MNR on what the national issues were and were the opposition them laid. Also, Paz's contacts and increased experience with the politics in Argentina also proved of use. Peron was continuing his search for a *third way* between capitalism and communism, as well as carrying successful influence over the labor force.

During World War II, in spite of the fact that Bolivia had declared war on the Axis powers, there were individuals whose sympathies continued in favor of the Nazis. It was against this history the U.S. was competing.

It was this connection from the past that Paz turned to for assistance to assist with the retraining of the military and the control of national strikes.

After WWII, Bolivia was one of those countries of resort to which Nazis fled. One notable Nazi was SS and Gestapo functionary, Klaus Barbie. By 1957, he had been identified as living in Bolivia. He resided in Cochabamba for over thirty years and had obtained Bolivian citizenship. He had become an influential member of the community. Peter McFarren, who, with his parents, was in Bolivia when we were, has done extensive personal research on Barbie.[65] I have already noted the SS training Paz's secret police received in which Barbie was probably involved.

While it may not seem significant to make reference to Germany in this history, Bolivian Methodism had numerous interactions with Germans, particularly those of the second wave of migration. Elena Eleska was one among others with whom we explored a business relationship; there were church members in La Paz, Cochabamba, and Santa Cruz of German descent; German schools were a serious competitor for students with the American Institutes; and the Jewish community was an important addition to the religious dimension of Bolivian society. No doubt, a residue of European fascism lingers on in Bolivian politics long after the end of Nazism in Germany.[66] The defeat of the Axis powers by the Allies moved along the process of Bolivia shedding its infatuation with the Axis.

---

[65] See also: Peter McFarren and Fadriquo Iglesias's book entitled, *The Devil's Agent: life, Times and Crimes of Nazi Klaus Barbie.*

[66] The Nazi objective was to gain influence over the countries of Argentina, Chile, Bolivia, Paraguay, and, in the last step, Brazil. For the Nazi infiltration of Latin America, see Jacon Ragone's *The Woman Who Smashed the Codes.*

# Chapter VIII

# November 1962–December 1968

### La Paz 1962–1964

In October 1962, as we were preparing to return to Bolivia, a major crisis developed regarding US–Cuban relations. A US U-2 spy plane in surveillance flights over Cuba had photographed nuclear missile sites being built by the Soviet Union. Obviously, any incident of this nature became a matter of importance for all of Latin America. By October 22, Kennedy had placed a ring of ships around Cuba as a naval blockade to prevent the arrival of further shipments from the USSR. In an address to the nation, Kennedy shared what was happening.

Our family plans were in place and we were returning to Bolivia. For thirteen days, the standoff was racking. Finally, the response by the Russians was the dismantling of the missile sites. The Russian ships with the missiles were allowed to return home. The incident, as we began our second term of service, was a reminder the Cold War could heat up again very quickly and in our backyard.

The furlough year had been one of full of different flows of information. There was a steady flow of news from Bolivia. This was mainly of an updating nature to keep me informed of developments. There was the flow of information I was directly gathering by visits to churches. A third was what might be considered personal improvement. That was the knowledge about my employer, the internal operations of the Board of Missions, and my skills development through the training experience at the NTL lab in Maine. The fourth stream of thought was more personal about my family. With so much travel for speaking engagements, I was away from my wife and children most of the ten months I had been in the States. I needed time to spend with them, my parents and brothers and sister, and their families.

At one time or another, one of these held the dominant position. As furlough ended, thoughts about the Methodist Church became more dominant. They were about the state of the Bolivian church and how I would fit into it after being away for almost a year.

By having over two hundred speaking engagements with groups wanting to hear about Bolivia, my thoughts flowed more in what had been accomplished and not enough about the future of the Bolivian Methodism. However, as the furlough was ending and we were planning our return to Bolivia, my thinking shifted to thinking about the future.

By being at a distance, I had a chance to look at Bolivia and the Methodist Church in a more reflective mode. The numerical growth and the geographic expansion of the church were suggesting how the church was changing.

Church growth was suggesting a change in the demographics of the membership of the church. One change coming was suggesting that while the leadership was mainly Spanish-speakers, membership growth was indicating that the Aymara-speaking and, to a lesser degree, the Quechua-speaking membership were becoming the majority. While the missionary tended to view the country as a whole, the historian Henderson and others always spoke of Bolivia as two countries. The MNR had taken that into account with the policies it had enunciated.

A second reality was related to the missionaries. With the Methodist family, there were three changing takings place: A) the missionary group was becoming more diverse with personnel from Japan, Brazil, Argentina, and Uruguay; B) the role of the missionary was changing. Missionaries were increasingly coming to Bolivia with technical skills, while missionaries who came as ordained clergy were moving from the parish into ministerial training activities or types of chaplaincies such as university student ministries; and C) the missionary vocation was changing from being a lifetime commitment to a short-term duration required to complete a task or function.

To the observant, Bolivian Methodism soon would be reaching another stage in developing as an institution. I was anxious to know what Bishop Barbieri, Jim Pace, Anibal Guzman, Adolfo Angeles, Mario Salazar, Gaston Pol, and others were thinking about the church. It would be important also to know what had developed in Bolivian politics. When we left Bolivia, it seemed like the MNR was fragmenting. The US news services carried little news about Bolivia. It would be good to know what was happening and how I would fit in.

We were very warmly received back to Bolivia. The Annual Conference met in the American Institute in Cochabamba. Now I could shut down some of the other areas of interest and place them on the back burner. It was time to give my full attention to my responsibilities in Bolivia.

The Lands of Decision program of the board which had given such a boast to the work in Bolivia with a large increase in personnel and significantly increased financial resources was over. The four-year period for the program ended in January 1961. There was a momentum that would continue, but we needed to be aware of the slacking off of support. The board was giving consideration to the urgent needs of mission work in other countries. Also, Murray was gone. The board arranged my itineration to step into those contacts. Murray had a lot of contacts and relationships that would be hard for any one person to fill. There were several commitments that would continue for a while but probably not indefinitely.

There was no replacement for the Lands of Decision program. Whatever happened would result from an effort by all of us. That meant building on contacts and cultivation for funding just to replace funding sources. The extensive contacts in Texas and Oklahoma seemed to indicate that some of our support was due to it being a conference-wide program such as that of the Southwest Texas Conference, requiring encouragement to continue. Some support was based on personal friendships that Murray had which, with his death, might become a softer source of support. The continuing cultivation of financial support will require an effort by missionaries from these two states.

However, the ultimate goal was self-sufficiency for an autonomous national church. The church in Bolivia was a long way from being able to continue to function anywhere near its current level based solely on the offerings collected on Sunday mornings in churches in Bolivia.

What this meant was that if the Bolivian church was going to reach anywhere near the goal of being self-supporting, it would need to find other funding sources in Bolivia in addition to the Sunday morning offerings. It was something that would not just happen but had to be planned for. It became one of my major considerations from day one back in Bolivia.

The missionary family had grown quite large. It was numbering well over ninety, with personnel from the U.S., Argentina, Uruguay, Japan, and Switzerland. The diversity of personnel was important. Diversity, while being a desirable condition, also can have negative consequences in the form of equality and fair treatment.

My experience as pastor of the Union Church in Cochabamba had also given me some insights into the experiences an American family goes through by being in a second cultural setting. Having been away almost a year, I could see signs at the Annual Conference where some familiar strains were showing which needed attention. Also, children of missionaries were developing into teenagers and young adults with changing needs. National pastors' families were growing which required opportunities for post-high school education. The conference as an organization would need to enlarge its sense of responsibility to include the whole family with its diverse needs.

Also, with the diversity of programs, the church had developed a category of lay workers in education, the medical field, and other vocational areas. In fairness, the church needed to develop forms of support in training and in retirement for these valuable workers. Vocational training programs existed for unordained church workers on the Altiplano and one in Montero. However, some form of continuing education to improve skills needed to be considered.

One of the things quite obvious to me when we returned was how the number of national pastors was increasing. Several had returned from Buenos Aires just before we left on furlough. Now Wesley Seminary was functioning as well as a school of Christian workers in the Altiplano. The need for additional missionaries from the U.S. would only be in those fields where, as yet, either Bolivian or personnel from other Latin American countries were not yet available. Regardless, it meant that positions ought to be filled conditionally until a trained Bolivian was available. Perhaps, short-term volunteers were part of the solution.

Already the church was making use of one form of short-term volunteer workers without committing personnel through the full-time missionary career path by requesting missionaries. It was taking place in Eastern Bolivia, especially in the colonies through the PAX men in the colonies from the Mennonite Central Committee. However, a new source appeared that might be a means of securing such personnel for other areas of work of the church.

In 1960, Murray directed me to attend to a request from five Perkins Seminary students from Southern Methodist University to see if I could provide them with work activities in the eastern district. The work team was coming to do jobs that would free up missionaries from tasks that others could do. Heading up the team was a young seminary student by the name of Bob Kochtitzky. Bob had owned paint store. Business was good. He was good at sales and making a good profit. However, he began to think that God was calling him to do something else with his life. He wasn't sure just what that might be. He sold his store in 1958 to be free from the "responsibilities of private enterprise." He said he saw it as God calling him out of the paint store rather than into some other business. Bob made arrangements to spend some months with a missionary in the Philippines from Jackson, Mississippi, Bob's hometown. It made a profound impression on him. Bob wrote about his experience:

> The uniqueness of missionaries lies not in a special kind of elevated status; rather it lies in the integrity of their humanity and their commitment in love and joy to a life

of service. Missionaries are different all right, but not in the way I had anticipated!⁶⁷

When he returned to Mississippi he decided to enroll in seminary. Three other students became impressed by Bob's experience and his thoughts about a program of short-term service by laypersons to support and free up persons committed to a full-time vocation in the church.

---

[67] Kochtitzky, Robert, *Laos – Laymen's Overseas Service* Occasional Bulletin, Vol. xvi, no. 11

Robert Boone Kochtitzky passed away peacefully on May 5, 2016, in Okeechobee, FL, Mississippi State University. With a business degree, he joined the air force during the Korean War. Upon completing his military service, he entered seminary at Southern Methodist University and received a Master of Theological Study. During the height of the civil rights struggle, he started an organization called LAOS or Laymen's Overseas Services to help place volunteers into service projects all over the world. During this time, he also served as one of the Mississippi Freedom Democratic Party *replacement* delegates to the 1968 Democratic National Convention. After his house was bombed by the Klan for his efforts on behalf of the civil rights movement, Bob moved his family and his organization to Baltimore, and then Washington, D.C. Bob embarked on a new mission, founding a group called Alternatives to highlight the over-commercialization of holidays and celebrations. Alternatives published an alternative celebrations catalogue designed to highlight new ways to commemorate birthdays and holidays. The catalogue eventually saw more than 150,000 copies printed and was featured nationally on the Phil Donahue Show. Bob and his family in the mid '70s founded a series of non-profit organizations aimed at improving the quality of life in Mississippi. He helped found the city-wide recycling system that is today the current city-run curbside recycling program. Also, he was involved in the creation of the city's first Green Habitat House in Jackson, MI. Later, he began to focus on environmental education issues. He founded the Mississippi 2020 Network (MS 2020) aimed at deploying 20/20 vision toward those environmental problems likely to damage the world by the year 2020. Under the auspices of MS 2020, he created the EcoScore Program; the Clean, Green, and Healthy Schools Project; and the Our World Discovery Project (later renamed the Growing Good Citizens Project). He was asked to serve on the U.S. Environmental Protection Agency's (EPA) National Advisory Committee on Environmental Education. A lifelong United Methodist, Bob was a member of both Wells and Galloway United Methodist Churches in Jackson (Obituary Clarion-Ledger, May 11, 2016).

A lawyer friend, Francis Stevens, urged Bob to visit Bolivia during the summer of 1962 before taking a team there. Jim Pace, the executive secretary of the Annual Conference met Bob and picked up on the plans in a concrete way. LAOS (Laymen's Overseas Service Inc.) was incorporated in 1962 as a non-profit corporation headquartered in Jackson, Mississippi. it was to be governed by an interdenominational board of directors. Bob realized that an acronym for Laymen's Overseas Service would easily be *laos* or the Greek word for *the people*. In other words, it would be a service to assist ordinary people to be in mission. "And in the conviction that the church abroad is critically hampered by a lack of trained personnel, a *matchmaker* (LAOS) seemed imperative to wed the need and the volunteer."[68]

The Bolivia Annual Conference continued to relate to Laymen's Overseas Services (LAOS) until 1968. During the preceding years, almost three hundred volunteers came to Bolivia, paying their own travel and covering their own support to work alongside personnel of the Bolivian church. In most cases, assisting with training of local personnel.

Soon after we returned to Bolivia, it was important to get a perspective on what was happening in other countries of Latin America, both in the Methodist Church as well as in politics in general. US hegemony continued over the areas, as aspects of the Cold War continued. The decade of President Roosevelt's Good Neighbor policy, which had generated a mood of goodwill among the countries of the Western Hemisphere, had rapidly changed with the advent of World War II as the United States took steps to close off the hemisphere from the rest of the world and especially the Axis powers. By its actions, it made clear to the countries of Latin America that they actually had little choice but to become more dependent on the United States. The US expectation was hemispheric solidarity. All of the countries of Latin America, with the exception of Chile and Argentina, broke or declared war on the Axis powers. The two countries remained neutral until shortly before the end of the war. Both Brazil and Mexico, on the other hand, sent troops to fight with the Allies.

During World War II, the U.S. expanded its involvement and influence throughout Latin America. The U.S. had become the major source of

---

[68] Kochtitzky. Ibid, 2.

manufactured goods and the primary market for Latin America. About 1950, relations between the U.S. and Latin America became tense, with the U.S. continuing to exert a strong influence over the area due to the Cold War.

By the time we arrived back in Bolivia in 1957, the tension between Bolivia and the U.S. was on the rise. In countries where reformers or modernizers were at work to bring about urgently needed changes, too frequently the U.S. misinterpreted their intentions and objectives undermining what should have been recognized as efforts of political and economic nationalism.

What was at the crux of the matter was an understanding of the means by which development could take place in countries of Latin America. The international financial aid sources were formed by capitalism. The U.S. made it clear these were the appropriate means to use. Most Latins saw their world from a different perspective with the choice not be solely between communism and capitalism. They felt attempts were being made and were concerned about the U.S.'s unwillingness to allow options to be explored. What they had experienced of capitalism was unacceptable because it took advantage of national resources without adequate reimbursement. Neither did they want to exchange one master for another in communism. There were many who saw continuing with the U.S. as simply maintaining a dependency relationship.

In 1952, the MNR-led revolution was not anti-American. In its early years, though, its leadership, especially Victor Paz Estenssoro, was considered to be leftist and placed under suspicion. Historians claim that the reason Bolivia was not treated as a communist takeover was due to the fact that there was not a significant US corporation involved in Bolivia who had the political means to gain Washington's ear, as was the case with Guatemala with the US corporation, the United Fruit Company.

In 1954, tensions between Argentina and the U.S. developed. It may have been due in part to the Argentinian position of neutrality in WWII. More than likely was the increasing disposition of Peron who explored a third way independent of the U.S. and Moscow. News sources covering Latin America tended to see any form of disagreement as being unacceptable to Washington and, therefore, bad news for the U.S.

On furlough, we constantly ran into questions concerning communism in Bolivia and in Latin America. With many North Americans, it seemed an obsession with them. Whether the question came directly or subtly, we had to deal with the current misunderstandings about politics in Latin America. The interpretation of events in Guatemala and Cuba as a communist takeover made it difficult to convey the significance of the revolution in Bolivia.

The dynamics of change were working in the overall relationships between the U.S. and the countries of Latin America and among the several countries individually.

It seemed that the election of Kennedy was hopeful. The heightened tensions during the Cuban missile crisis, while a sign the Cold War was not over, seemed to be out of step with what was Kennedy's policy position of moving beyond a world divided in at least two camps.

In 1963, in an address at American University, a Methodist university, Kennedy urged Americans to reexamine Cold War stereotypes. He called for a strategy of peace that would make the world safe for democracy. In addition, Kennedy took two actions to contribute to peace. He established a *hotline* between the Kremlin and the White House for a more immediate reaction to any tension. Kennedy signed with other nations the Limited Nuclear Test Ban Treaty on July 25, 1963. These seemed to be signs of hope for better relations.

These hopes were short-lived. Just about a year after our return to Bolivia, a tragic event occurred. It was the assassination of President John F. Kennedy. About noon on the twenty-second of November 1963, I went for my customary walk down to the Prado from our office on Landaeta Street. The first Bolivian I came upon voluntarily expressed how deeply sorry she was. I could not grasp what she meant even though I understood what she said. It was only a moment when a second person said about the same thing. I was in total ignorance. I couldn't quite comprehend what I was being told. I asked him to repeat what he had said. "Your president has been killed." In disbelief I went on to the little shop I always visited. The owner, whom I knew well, told me more of the details. President Kennedy was visiting Dallas. While riding in an open convertible with his wife, he was shot several times and had died as a result of his wounds.

In disbelief, I turned and hurried up the hill to my office first and then home. Nat Barber had called the office to tell Ed the news. Her reaction had been similar to most of the Americans in Bolivia. She wrote afterward:

> As I was working with a doctor, as usual, someone knocked and opened the door to blurt out the news. My first reaction was that it was a mistake. All of Bolivia mourned. Everyone was especially considerate to us Americans. Flags were flown at half-mast and radio stations played classical music for three days. This tragedy would change our nation forever, something I didn't realize until we returned to the states in 1967.[69]

One could have hardly imagined the impact Kennedy's death would have on the citizens of another country. They had taken it as a personal loss. Their grief was real. Their expressions of sympathy were genuine. For one long moment, we were one family.

Ed and Natalie Barber, missionaries transferred from Chile before we arrived in Bolivia, were on furlough at the same time as we were. In fact, they were in Evanston, Illinois, for studies. Ed was assigned to the conference office as secretary of administration and as chaplain at the American clinic. Nat was the new editor of *Highland Echoes,* an English newsletter to a mailing list of about eight thousand.

This meant our two families had opportunity to be in touch more frequently. Our son John was about the age of their son, Mark. The two boys got along well and became frequent companions. The two enjoyed the freedom to explore the hospital. Much to my horror, it was reported to me that a patient having surgery with a local anesthesia while lying on the operating table looked up to the skylight overhead to see the faces of two boys staring down at him.

---

[69] Barber, Natalie, *Passport to Faith*, 2003, p. 66

I heard that Frank and Bessie Beck were being invited to attend the fiftieth anniversary of the founding of Ward College in Buenos Aires in November 1963. I wrote to them asking if they would return to Bolivia for six months to fill the gap we were having with the loss of Dr. Tatum.

In many respects, Dr. Beck was considered the father of medical work in Bolivia. Frank Beck was an educational missionary who arrived in Bolivia in 1912 to join the staff of the American Institute in La Paz. A year later, Bessie joined the missionary staff to marry Frank. Frank came to the conclusion after several years of teaching that it was difficult when someone was sick and hungry to concentrate on learning. When a furlough came, Frank enrolled in Northwestern University medical school. Bessie cared for three small children and found time to work in one year of studies at the University of Chicago. They occupied an apartment for missionaries on the campus. With financial help from the Board of Missions, they finished their studies. The had retired by the time we arrived on the field.

> The first medical work of the Methodist Church in Bolivia was started by Df. Charles Foster and his wife, a nurse. George McBride, directory of the Methodist school in La Paz, influenced an Italian-American miller, Antonion Chirioto, to buy a farm at Guatajata as a mission to the Indians. Dr. and Mrs. Foster joined Rev. and Mrs. Hugh Wenburg in establishing the mission farm in 1911. In addition to the medical service the farm ran a school and church.
>
> After the Methodist Centenary, a relief effort after WWI in 1919, the Board of Missions projected opening Methodist hospitals in five capital cities in L.A. One was to be in La Paz and another in Lima, Peru. The first hospital to operate was the one in Lima. Methodist Bolivian girls were sent there for nurses training. One of the first to graduate and return to La Paz was Lia Penaranda, the daughter of Pastor Nestor and Angelica Penaranda, who played an important role in translating for Dr. Beck on his trips to the Altiplano.

On his return trip in 1963 he oversaw the construction of a clinic in Ancoraimes built as the Dr. Beck Clinic. Years before, Frank had started the medical work on the Altiplano. He traveled on a motorcycle with a sidecar with Pastor Penaranda. Frank had delivered about five thousand babies. When he retired, there was such an outpouring of love from the Bolivian people. "The front of the hospital was decorated with flowers and streamers. Dignitaries and staff stood outside to welcomes them with smiles and abrazos (hugs)."[70] He was awarded the Condor of the Andes for his contribution to the people of Bolivia. Beside him through it all was Bessie Dunn Beck, who had a doctorate in sociology, while Frank had earned a medical degree. Their daughter, Miriam Beck Knowles, had founded the first school of nursing in Bolivia, alongside the Methodist Hospital. When the government started a school of nursing, as a faculty in the University of San Andres in La Paz, a graduate of the Methodist School of Nursing was its first director.

Frank and Bessie Beck were persons of great compassion and greater faith. In the American clinic in La Paz, Dr. Beck treated those who spoke Spanish and lived in a more or less modern world. On the Altiplano, Dr. Beck treated those belonging to the ethnolinguistic Aymara group who never knew a doctor before and died due to the lack of the simplest knowledge of hygiene and infections.

Rachel and I arrived in Bolivia in the fall of 1957. Bill Jack was our physician. The following is a list of directors of the Methodist Hospital:

| | |
|---|---|
| Bill Jack Marshall | 195–1959 furlough |
| Pablo Monti | 1960– |
| Bill Jack Marshall | 1961–1964 |
| Pablo Monti | 1965– |
| Thorburn Thompson | 1966–1969 |
| Lindsay Smith | 1969–1974 |

What was happening in the decade of which I am speaking is that the medical program of Methodism in Bolivia took a major step forward. First, it expanded geographically to the frontiers of Methodist growth:

---

[70]  Ibid., 66.

| | | |
|---|---|---|
| Enrique Cicchetti | 1961 | Caranavi |
| Teresa Silvera | 1960 | Cochabamba |
| Silva Sanchez | 1969 | Santa Cruz colonies |
| Pablo Monti | 1961 | Santa Cruz |
| James Alley | 1964 | Montero |

Medical personnel sent by the Women's Division: Ernestine Harmon arrived in 1957, and Rosella Bonorden and Margaret Toothman arrived in 1958.

The medical practice in Bolivia had to adjust to conditions very distinct in each in geographic region. The Altiplano, the first rural environment into which Methodism medical work extended, was a high-altitude plateau with harsh weather conditions especially problematic with respiratory diseases such as whooping cough, TB, typhus, and gastrointestinal conditions. The Yungas and Santa Cruz/Montero areas are much lower in elevation with a warmer semitropical climate. The diseases encountered are malaria, yellow fever, and intestinal parasites. In areas of transition such as the colonies, the arrival of new residents lack natural immunities or knowledge of sanitation and personal hygiene. Populations living in valleys, such as Cochabamba, experienced health issues related to waterborne diseases, nutritional and contagious infections.

One can only imagine the importance of a public health program to provide the basic information about how factors in the environment affect one's health. The Indian from the Altiplano who came to the tropics to take up land must learn from hard experience the lessons concerning elements in the environment that are making him sick. Once, he could drink from a stream fed by melt snows. Now he lives in the tropics where his drinking water contains parasites or where a bite can be from a malaria-carrying mosquito.

In 1900, the records of the Ministry of Health indicate that there were 142 doctors practicing medicine in Bolivia. The Ministry reports that in 1955 there were 759 registered doctors and seventy-nine licensed midwives attending a population of approximately three million persons.[71] A 1953

---

[71] Archivo Nacional ANB; Presidencia de la Republica, PR 1659, 23

report indicated that the entire medical profession was serving on one-third of the population.[72] In 1960, the doctor-patient ratio was 1:3,700; in Mexico it was 1:1800; and in Cuba it was 1:1200.[73]

The Methodist medical program went through a significant change during the 1960s. Absolute poverty was rampant everywhere. The type of agriculture governed by elevation and climate, however, determined nutritional diet. The practice increasingly became more focused on public health education. The emphasis has been on the control of infectious diseases, improved nutrition, and better environmental sanitation through education.

During the six months Dr. and Mrs. Beck were back in Bolivia in 1963, the head of medical work for the Board of Missions visited Bolivia. As part of his visit, I took him to Acoraimes to see the small five-bed clinic there and to meet Dr. Beck. It was an opportunity for Dr. Beck to share his dream of a new clinic with staff at the board who would need to approve it. The discussions for a new hospital were progressing well when we were interrupted. A truck carrying numerous passengers on top of its load had tipped over into Lake Titicaca as it took a curve in the road. The truckload of cargo came down on the passengers and pinned them under the water. Among the passengers, there were many dead and twenty-two injured. They were rushed to the clinic. The small clinic was overwhelmed.[74] After triage, the injured waited on the floor, filled the chairs, and stretched before the fireplace in the living room of the doctor's cottage. Whatever space was available was filled with a body. The wives of the doctors built a fire to dry clothes, served hot coffee, and made the injured as comfortable as they could while they waited to be seen by a doctor. I was drafted to be the anesthesiologist. I was instructed to place cotton over the patient's nose and mouth and pour drops of ether on it. Several of the men had been chewing coca. They were already immune to some pain but now also immune to the ether. Needless to say, the board medical officer needed little convincing about the need for a hospital in Ancoraimes.

---

[72]

[73] Eckstein, 1982:82+

[74] A personal experience also reported in the *History of Methodist Medical Work in Bolivia*, Bessie Beck PhD, 1974, page 65

The medical program of the Bolivia Conference was well launched for the years to come. It ran three-month training programs for rural parteras (midwives) and nine-month training programs for auxiliary nurses. There were hospitals in La Paz, Ancoraimes, and Montero, with outpost clinics and mobile clinics. To supplement the missionary and Bolivia staff, there were visiting medical teams from the Carolinas and Tennessee, medical doctors, dentists, and nurses who came through the LAOS and Andean Rural Health (Curamericas) programs. Short-term personnel such as Jim Beck, Dr. and Mrs. Brooks Taylor, and Henry Perry went on to perform valuable research on rural public health issues.

## A Self-Sustaining Church

As I have already mentioned, my itineration to churches in the Southwest led me to feel that with the end of the Lands of Decision effort and the death of Murray Dickson and, incidentally, the loss of Nova from the field, fundraising would be a consideration. The objective was, however, to build a base of local income so the church would not be dependent on funds for others.

One of the obvious possible sources of local income for the church would be a business based on Bolivian handicrafts. The manufacture and sale of items of traditional or typical design in cloth, wood, or stone was a growing market area. Bolivia has some very attractive apparel items, which are handmade, using local materials such as llama or alpaca wool, and weaving was a skill common in the indigenous communities of the highlands.

The possibility to become involved with the production of woven items presented itself to us. A woman by the name of Elena Aleska approached me about the possibility of the Methodist Church assuming the responsibility for a business she had started. I had not known her, but she was a native of Cochabamba and was well acquainted with the American Institute as well as other activities in the valley.

Several conversations were held to explore what Madam Aleska had in mind. It became clear that she was a very intelligent, sophisticated person. She was advanced in years and was looking for a way to see her work continued after her demise. The vision she had for her business was not simply to make money but to focus on developing the artistic and cultural aspects of life for the producer and for the buyer.

The business she was seeking to find lodgment for was a successful weaving industry located in the Cochabamba Valley for Quechua-speaking women. These women would work at two weaving centers to make woven apparel, such as ponchos, hats, bags, and other items. The weaving centers provided the looms and material. They also provided training for the women. More importantly, the centers suggested designs and provided quality control. The items produced by the women were very desirable items that could be sold on the world market. Madam Eleska had established marketing outlets in Europe and the U.S. The woman could work on her own schedule; meaning, when she had time available. The finished product was purchased from the weaver who was paid in cash. The weaver was relieved of the responsibility of marketing.

> Elena Elesaka was born in Vienna, Austria, on May 16, 1885. Her name was Lene Schneider. She had Jewish-Austrian parents. Her father was Sigmud Schneider, a painter. Elena started art studies in Paris which she continued in Munich, Paris, and Amsterdam. In 1910, she married Ludwig Kainer, and worked as a doctor, painter, graphic designer, poster artist, and stage designer. They traveled in the world of artists and intellectuals. Schneider-Kainer made her debut as an artist with an exhibit of some fifty oil paintings in Berlin in 1917. Her most outstanding years were 1919–1922, enjoying acclaim in Berlin. In 1926, they were divorced. She began an extended odyssey with Bernhard Kellermann, a poet. They travelled by donkey or caravan, visiting Russia, Persia, India, Burma, Thailand, Vietnam, Tibet, and Hong Kong. She painted, photographed, and sketched her impressions which appeared regularly in Berlin magazines. She did not return to Germany due to the rise of Hitler. She had successful exhibits in Barcelona, Copenhagen, New York, and Philadelphia. In 1954, she settled in Cochabamba under the name Elena Eleska. At eighty-six, she died on June 15, 1971 (See Wikipedia and Museum of Jewish History).

The conversations took place over several months. They involved Madam Eleska's lawyer and business center managers. When architect plans were drawn for the COSMOS building, space was indicated for an arts and crafts store, as well as a bookstore at street level to reach a local market as well as tourist trade. After over a year of conversation I was notified that a different disposition had been made for the business Madam Aleska had started. It was a great disappointment. This meant we needed to continue to search for local sources.

In 1961, the conference had approved a project of a student center for Laz near the University of San Andres. On furlough, the First United Methodist Church of Wichita Falls, Texas was prepared to provide a sum of about $30,000 for such a center. A property was located on Avenida Arce just above Plaza Estudiantil near the Hotel Sucre. It was an old residence now in bad shape that could be fixed up for students.

The site seemed to be ideal for an income property, as well as church-related activities. One of the church members, who was an architect, had designed several church buildings. I called on Noel Salazar, Mario's younger brother, to discuss how we might use the property for a mixed purpose building. After several exchanges of ideas, a draft was developed of a building that would have a center entrance with two shops, one on each side of the entrance. The first several floors would be for a student center and church offices. A twelve-story building was discussed with an apartment on the top floor for the bishop or church head, whatever the title.

Months were involved with all of the contacts and conversations that needed to take place. The first was to reach an agreement with the Board of Missions that the student center project could be changed. Then permission had to be sought from the donor church that their contribution be used for a modified purpose. Noel, on his part, needed to develop more specific plans as well as the necessary change of use of property agreement from the city. Also, a major issue would be the fact that the back of the building fronts on another street but actually one story below street level. One of Noel's first concerns was the type of retaining wall necessary to maintain the stability of the building with vehicle traffic passing on two sides of the building. The biggest obstacle to overcome was the cost.

The cost of a multistory building was quite different from the original project of an older resident being remodeled for student use. In this regard, the church replied very soon that they would not be making an additional contribution to the project. The board was aware of what the revised plans would involve and were reluctant to make any commitment until they had more information.

In brief, several other sources were being explored without a definitive resolution before my term ended in 1968. The projected building was to be called COSMOS. The plan for the layout was that there would be two commercial shops on the street level. The thought was one would be for Bolivian handicrafts and the other a Methodist bookstore for religious publications. A floor would be set aside for a ministry for students. The other floors would be allocated to church office and at least one residence. Among the space for the office would be adequate meeting rooms for groups wishing to meet. The rest of the building would be income property; the returns after maintenance and upkeep would be designated to a retirement fund for ordained clergy.

Such a building would give the church visibility in the country, as well as serve needs of the church in several ways.

## Methodism's Commitment to Education in Bolivia

The fifth of the policy emphasis of the MNR on assuming power in 1952 was education. Opportunities were presenting themselves for Methodism to expand its own school system due to the many requests by communities wanting a school. It was also expanding, as there were increasing opportunities to influence the government's school system.

It hardly needs to be said that Methodism was greatly interested in education. That was a characteristic inherited from John Wesley who held education as of highest importance. American Methodism fell into step and started academies and schools wherever it went. The circuit riders carried Bibles and other books in their saddlebags. As the church matured, every Annual Conference was asked to start a college. It was also an imperative of Methodism that its clergy be educated.

Bishop Taylor, the missionary bishop of early Methodism, recruited laymen and laywomen to be teachers in schools. He then planted in almost every port when he circled South America from Brazil around the cape to Ecuador. The first Methodist mission post in Bolivia was a school Bishop Taylor planted in Antofagasta when it was part of Bolivia.

In 1906, when Methodism returned to Bolivia, it did so by starting a school in La Paz in 1906, and then another in Cochabamba in 1912.

The two institutes were only the beginning. Schools were opened on the Altiplano and Trinidad. These were augmented by a vocational school in Ancoraimes and another in Montero. A school of nursing started very soon after the medical work began. And a girls' school was begun in Ancoraimes.

A ministry with students was started in the form of a student hostel at the university in Sucre and a ministry to students in Warisata. Plans were on the drawing board for a student center in La Paz for the students at the public university of San Andres to be included in the plans for the new COSMOS building.

However, as Methodism itself was moving toward maturity, it was not just the quantity of schools but the quality of the education being offered in the schools that would be important in the long run. I sought advice from my brother, Dr. Lloyd McCleary, Chair of the Department of Graduate Studies of the College of Education of the University of Utah. He indicated that in the funding agreement with the U.S. it would be possible to secure assistance through grants from the State Department.

Lloyd undertook a series of visits to Bolivia in order to visit Methodist schools and offer advice and counsel on school administration to school directors. Mario Salazar and Gaston Pol were closely involved with Lloyd. The emphasis was to develop leadership in order to improve the quality of education being offered in Methodist schools. He assisted several educators to receive graduate degrees. Both missionaries and Bolivians benefited from his assistance. In addition to Gaston Pol, Gary Fritz, Martha Ovando, and Absail Antello, and Dale Good were among those who continued graduate studies in the field of education leading to advanced degrees.

Beginning in 1963, arrangements were made with Dr. Fred Prof, psychologist on the faculty of the University of Texas, Houston, to come with Dr. McCleary on a trip to Bolivia. Dr. Prof had agreed to do family counseling with missionaries who were having adjustment problems with working conditions in Bolivia or marriage counseling.

These arrangements were made because several missionaries had indicated such services would be helpful to them. The purpose of this agreement with Dr. Prof was meant to assist individuals to live more fulfilling lives. The Board of Missions was not involved in the agreement. The first trip was an introductive one. It was to acquaint Dr. Prof with Bolivia and the missionary community. Information about Dr. Prof was circulated to missionaries about how he could be contacted. From that point on, all contact was to be handled directly with Dr. Prof. Dr. Prof scheduled several trips to Bolivia. The conference office was not involved in any way other than to be advised when Dr. Prof was present in the country. Dr. Prof continued his services for over three years before he terminated the agreement.

Soon after our residence in La Paz, I became acquainted with the La Paz representative of the Wycliffe Translators, David Farah. Wycliffe Bible Translators is an interdenominational organization for the purpose of translating the Bible into every language being spoken around the world. There were several groups, as I have mentioned, of an interdenominational nature with which we worked. Many came to Bolivia just before or soon after the '52 revolution.

David Farah ran the La Paz office, while others related to the organization held field positions around the country. David became a good friend, and his and our children enjoyed each other's company. We were interested, of course, with the Wycliffe organization because of its efforts to make the Bible available. Often Bible translation first required reducing a spoken to a written language by producing an alphabet. In Bolivia, Wycliffe identified, in addition to Quechua and Aymara, some twenty-eight other indigenous languages in usage. This reduction of language was among the tribes or groupings in the eastern lowlands. Our frontier of movement was into areas occupied by these language groups.

Bolivian Methodism was expanding through Trinidad on the Mamore River which formed part of the Amazon Basin. In each of these areas, the church was advancing toward or into areas of a new indigenous people of the eastern lowlands.

> Wycliffe USA was founded in 1942 by William Cameron Townsend. Townsend gave his new organization the name Wycliffe after John Wycliffe, who was responsible for the first complete English translation of the whole Bible into Middle English. The idea of such an organization quickly spread to other countries. The mission statement for Wycliffe reads, to "serve with the global body of Christ to advance Bible translation and work together so people can encounter God through his Word." By the end of the year 2020, of the estimated seven thousand active languages today, the Bible, or portions of it, have been translated into over three thousand four hundred. Wycliffe claims responsibility for translation into over seven hundred languages. Not only was it a matter of helping preliterate people learn to read and write, it meant developing a written language including an alphabet. Wycliffe also collaborates with the Deaf Bible Society to develop sign languages.

This meant that our contacts with Wycliffe would be increasingly valuable.

In the Beni on trips to Trinidad, we would travel the Mamore River and others on the boat owned and operated by the Methodist Church. On one such trip we gave the boat a name. Since its purpose was to evangelize communities which existed along the banks of the river, we thought an appropriate name would be *Vangie,* The boat was an important means of communication. It carried passengers, it brought foodstuffs, and it brought medicines into very isolated communities. On one trip we visited a community where a child had been killed by a jaguar. The men of the village had to find it and kill it because it would return to hunt. While there, they returned with the dead animal and skinned it, giving me the skin to bring back as a gift from the village (in red on the map).

In another trip into the Beni, I went with the pastor to visit several isolated towns that required we travel by plane. These little villages had cut landing strips to use. However, they had not cut the grass short enough, causing a drag on the wheels so the plane had difficulty in gaining sufficient ground speed to take off. To ensure we would be able to take off, the pilot took only one passenger with him at a time. He flew to the next village and made a return trip for the next passenger. By ferrying us out one by one, we were able to take the rest of the trip.

The Methodist boat was one of a few boats that travelled these rivers which were the primary means of transportation. It took days to make a round trip. We would tie up the boat by 4:00 p.m. to have an early meal cooked over a campfire, then hurry into the hammocks with netting to avoid the swarms of mosquitos.

The missionary fellowship in La Paz was an informal gathering of those who cared to be involved. It had no formal structure or agenda other than as a time of fellowship among missionaries of any religious group in La Paz. David Farah and wife, Wycliffe, were regular attenders. Another couple were the Hazen parents, Canadian Baptists who worked at their radio station, La Cruz del Sur (the Southern Cross). It was at these gatherings we heard of the developments in the work of others. The denomination seemed to be a small one. The mission in Bolivia was always operating on a careful budget. It did not have anything like our Lands of Decision effort to rescue it. The work of the station was considered important for the Protestant community in Bolivia. Among its many contributions was its contribution to outreach the illiterates.

In 1964, Methodists became concerned for the future of the station and decided to support the work of the station. In exchange, the Baptists invited me to service the station's board of directors, which I did. Evidently, when they heard news that other denominations held their mission work in high regard, the Canadian Baptist board was led to work harder at securing adequate support for the station.

Bolivian Methodism began in the formal classroom environment. But from that base, it began to spread into other pedagogical methodology. The initial transition was to brief seminars around a specific issue or topic.

In 1960, Dr. Gerald Harvey, the education consultant from the Board of Missions, visited Bolivia. Dr. Harvey came specifically to offer a short training program for Sunday School teachers. His field was Christian Education. His specific skill was in the preparation of lay persons with little training in Christian education. The short-term seminar was a method used with a variety of topics: child care, nutrition, sanitation, personal hygiene, food preservation, seed and fertilizer, and food preparation.

A longer training period was used for more complex issues. A training course of three months had been noted for the training of rural midwives. Funds from USAID provided each graduate with a bag with basic equipment. A nine- month training program for auxiliary nurses.

Another form of education the church made use of might be called *modeling*. This was used widely in the lowland areas by the use of rural teams. In the Montero area, individuals become a part of a new settlement or colony. The purpose would be for them to serve as a resource or model to be emulated by the settler. They would be resourced through a monthly gathering where they could share information and gain new skills themselves.

A modification of this type of modeling was used in an urban setting in 1967 by the Sherrills. In January 1967, John and Elizabeth (Libby) Sherrill, along with their three children, Elizabeth, John Scott, and Donn, arrived in Bolivia beginning what was to be a year of living in Latin America. John taught the basics of journalism that would help get stories in the news. Libby taught writing inspirational stories about church members. These sessions were open to individuals from any of the Protestant groups who were interested. The Sherrills worked for Guideposts, a monthly magazine full of short stories. Guideposts was starting a program of writers' workshops, and John and Tibby were their primary instructors. Following a year in Latin America, they were to spend a year in Africa.

> John and Tibby met onboard a ship enroute to Europe where both were going to Geneva, Switzerland to study. They were married in December, 1947. Un 1952, John was hired as associate editor at *Guideposts* magazine. *Guideposts* had started in 1945 primarily as a guide to help service personnel adjust back into civilian life after the war. Begun with a subscription list of 800, it had grown to 300,000 by 1952. (In 2018 it was 2 million.)

John and Tibby began by offering a seminar-type program. Once they had introduced the topic, they offered skills. However, from that point on, they offered individual counsel and assistance on an individual basis. It proved to be a very effective method of training through initial sharing, and then by ongoing support as the person senses the need for it.

## Methodism and Unions

The policies of the MNR encouraged first the formation of rural syndicates or unions through the agrarian reform legislation. The miners were already organized. These labor organizations grew in importance as they assumed a political role. The COMIBOL, organization of miners, was the most powerful one. Methodism had not been as activity in mining communities. Methodism's strength was among the agricultural workers, especially on the Altiplano and in the Cochabamba Valley.

A Methodist became an early leader of the unionization of agricultural workers on the Altiplano. Factionalism existed among communities on the Altiplano which created problems for the leadership of the union. Felipe Flores was elected the executive secretary of the Campesinos union. Efforts were made by several pastors to provide Felipe with different forms of support. In conversation with Felipe, I was aware of his need for not just moral support but help with transportation and personal security. When I heard, it did not come as a surprise to receive the news that Felipe had been gunned down on the steps of the Ministerio de Asuntos Campesinos (Ministry of Rural Affairs).

It seemed important for the Methodist Church to be more involved to protect the lives of its members as they offer witness through the work they have chosen to do.

It also was occurring that Methodists were occupying positions in unions because they were able to read and write, and also not inclined to be heavy drinkers. It seemed that while the community were opposed to being Protestant, they also respected the moral lifestyle held by a Protestant.

In reflecting on the situation in which Methodists would be increasingly placed, it seemed that, as a church, we ought to be doing more to support them with the responsibilities they were asked to assume. Because of the political nature of unions in Bolivia, I felt it inappropriate to seek any form of assistance from an American union. This ruled out asking the Board of Missions since they would turn to an entity such as the AF of L or the

CIO.⁷⁵ Regarding help, I asked a friend, an American who headed the Lutheran World Federation based in Geneva. His suggestion was someone from the chaplains in industry in the Ruhr Valley of France.

With his help, arrangements were made with the Reformed Church of France. They selected and sent an ordained minister who worked in the field of industrial unions for one year. This was not to be a high-level program or the general public would misunderstand what the Methodists might be up to. Pastors in La Paz and in other areas were contacted to supply the conference office with the names of active church members who also belonged to and participated in a union. From the names provided, less than twenty names were selected. These persons were approached to see if they would like to be involved in a training program about the functioning of a union. No large meeting was convened. Small group sessions were held with three or four persons only. After about six months, the program was concluded on the grounds that Bolivian unions were of a distinctly different nature than those in Europe. The pastor felt he had communicated what was most useful information he was able to offer. Conversations with the persons involved seemed to indicate they had been given information that brought them to a level of confidence to have made the effort worthwhile.

We moved from the residence across the driveway from the large building used by the staff from the Altiplano during a visit to the city. The lake house had served many purposes and was now divided into apartments. Our move was a short one; just about a block away on a dead-end street. Our move freed up a house on the campus for school staff. It placed us on a more secluded street.

Early in 1964 I received a call from the Casa Quemada asking if I would have the courtesy of coming to the office of the president that afternoon. It was not common nor was it unusual that I should receive such a request. I had met with President Paz on several occasions, and we had had expensive conversations. For such visits I had been instructed to enter by a side door rather than the front office. He came to the point of the request for my visit. He was anticipating an attempted coup by the military and needed to leave

---

[75] Thomas Field sheds more light on the role of the AFL=CIO in labor movements in *Union Busting as Development: Transnationalism, Empire and Kennedy's Secret Labor Program for Bolivia*, September 10, 2019

the country as soon as it could be arranged. He was asking if there might be a legitimate reason for his travel. As we visited, he was confident that a general, who was loyal to him, would be able to deal with the matter. However, it was best to avoid complications if he were out of the country. He did not wish his plans to be handled by his office or anyone in his administration because he was not sure in whom he could place full confidence.

A ham radio had been set up in the master bedroom of our new home. The purpose was so that urgent family matters for missionaries could be dealt with quickly. My thought was to contact Methodist universities where the president might be received to discuss conditions in Latin America. Through a friend, I was able to arrange phone patches to the office of the president of three Methodist universities. The school year was in process. It would be fortunate if such an arrangement could be made. Within twenty-four hours, I had affirmative responses from all three. I was able to indicate to the president that invitations had been extended with contact names and phone numbers. The following day the newspaper announced that the president had been invited to a lectureship in the U.S. that would take him to three universities, and it was assumed he might be out of the country for the next ten days.

In a matter of a day, I was called by Ambassador Henderson to come to his office as soon as I could. Needless to say, Henderson was extremely angry with me for making such arrangements without his knowledge. He indicated that the State Department should have known in order to provide Secret Service protection, as well as other courtesies of the State Department. I was told that an itinerary and arrangements for a head of state were the responsibilities of the State Department which he represented. Of course, I offered my apologies for not being more considerate. I knew Doug Henderson well. They attended Union Church. I had not expected such a strong reaction to Paz's trip. In a matter of about ten days, Paz returned. He called me to visit him. This conversation was quite different from the one with Ambassador Henderson. He told of how well he had been received at each university. He had also received a rather large honorarium from each. He also indicated that the matter which had been the cause of his trip had been successfully dealt with by a loyal general.

In a matter of a few months, I received a similar call. This time it was for assistance with a shorter time span and limited to some isolated location in Bolivia. He became a guest on the Methodist boat to visit villages on the Mamore River. The news coverage reported a successful visitation to constituencies in the Beni.

## Eucalyptus Visit

One of my responsibilities was to report to Bishop Barbieri the status and extension of the work of the church. This required almost a constant schedule of travel to some parts of Bolivia. One of the more unusual ones was a visit to Eucalyptus.

One of the new congregations was in another area of the Altiplano. It was in a small town called Eucalyptus. To give a clearer impression of the town, it needs to be said it was not named because of the prominence of trees. Rather, its name came from the fact it was a siding on the railroad where eucalyptus timber was off-loaded for use in the mines.

I understand that members of *El Redentor* Church began to visit Eucalyptus, whether for evangelistic purposes or because of family relations was not clear. Around 1956, they took on a more formal assignment to conduct Bible studies in Eucalyptus.

The congregation here was started by Daniel Marconi, a local general store owner. It was his custom to come to La Paz on weekends to buy stock for his store. He gave me the impression his relation to the Methodists began casually. One Sunday he walked past El Redentor Church where he heard singing. He went in, sat in the back of the church, and stayed for the whole service. Back in Eucalyptus, he shared with his family and friends what he had heard. Regardless of the exact way it began, Daniel and the Marconi family became the nucleus of a congregation. By 1957, the gathered group became a more formal congregation. Adolfo Angles, pastor of La Reforma, was assigned for pastoral oversight.

In 1958, it became an organized church named Bethany Methodist Church, with Cleto Zambrana assigned as pastor.

The way I met Daniel was on one of his visits to the city; he stopped by the conference office. He asked if I would visit Eucalyptus. It was a congregation, I put on my list of places to visit soon. When a visit was arranged, I learned that Eucalyptus was located between the towns of Silencio (Silence) and Soledad (Loneliness) which begins to tell you something about the town. As with other parts of the Altiplano that I knew, it was a barren, forlorn area.

I arrived on Saturday and was entertained by the Marconi family. Their store was the only building of two stories in the town. They lived over the store. I believe I was given the family bedroom. It was typical weather on the Altiplano. It was a cold windswept evening. There were seven homemade blankets on the bed, which accounted for warmth, but the weight of the homemade blankets made it difficult to sleep.

The morning service at which I preached was in a room crowded with people. Following the service, there were two weddings. After the weddings, I baptized their children. For lunch, there were two wedding parties in the enclosed yards of the families involved. Several of us moved from one wedding party to the other. The music, dancing, and food were part of a very lively atmosphere. About 4:00 p.m. we were interrupted by a visit from three men. They had heard that a clergy was in town. They had come to see if I would conduct a funeral for the wife of one of the men. She had died on Saturday. They wished to bury her within twenty-four hours. There was a casket maker in town but no doctor. Would I be willing to go to the cemetery with them?

It was already late afternoon. The sun was beginning to go down. The cold evening air would soon be very penetrating. As we walked about a mile to the cemetery outside of town some distance, I talked with the husband. He was a young man, certainly less than thirty years old. They had been married several years. She had been sickly the last several years. He had sold his herd to pay for cures to no avail.

The mood, for me, had changed so quickly, from a festive party to a funeral procession. The darkening sky and increasing cold conditions contributed to how we were feeling. Juan Lechin had been growing more influential in leading the miners to a political position approximating communism.

We continued walking. I commented to the young man that there seemed to be some justification of the increasing influence of communism. Much to my surprise, he spoke out quickly, saying he was vehemently opposed to what I had said. In spite of his situation, he was convinced that communism did not hold the answer for what Bolivia needed. I returned to La Paz, having been allowed the privilege to share moments with families who were rejoicing and other families deep in sorrow. The weekend had been packed with emotional experiences: the lovely Marconi family; the singing of the congregation in Aymara; the meaningful weddings and baptisms; the sorrowful grief of a young husband; and the political analysis were conditions would dictate something different. How much I learned in one weekend.

Etelvina Marconi became my secretary at the conference center. She had come to La Paz and taken a course at a secretarial school. Some years later I heard she had become involved in politics and held the post of deputy mayor of La Paz.

## Paz Out, Barrientos In

Our life was seriously disrupted in 1964 by the events leading to an end to MNR rule of twelve years. It began over the issue of Cuba.

One of the major external factors influencing US–Bolivian relations was the Cuban revolution in 1959. The Johnson Administration was frustrated with Paz's refusal to break with Cuba. It was clear in the beginning that Castro was not communist nor was he leading a Marxist revolution. It was a nationalistic revolution to take back Cuba from the dominance of mafia, gambling, and prostitution. Due to the negative impact Castro's revolt had on US business interests, they appealed to the US government for protection.[76] The ultimate result was Castro had to turn to the only source of financial assistance available to him which was Moscow. It then became a game of Cuba attempting to maintain a degree of independence.

---

[76] Absentee ownership of land and businesses was beyond imagination. The Illinois farm family that owned the five hundred acres my wife's family worked in Illinois owned 12,0000 acres in Cuba. In Florida, I met an American who owned a half dozen auto repair parts stores across the island.

However, the Cuban revolution colored all of the US State Department's relationships throughout Latin America. The threat for the U.S. was the fear that Cuba would become a model of Latin American communism for the other countries of the hemisphere; in other words, *the domino effect* would occur. The old strategy of *sending in the marines* was not popular nor did it bring desired results. The U.S. had turned to providing the Bolivian revolution (MNR) funding to the point of Bolivia became the largest recipient of US aid in Latin America.[77] At the same time, its strategy included using every influence it had to isolate Cuba in order to cause the failure of Castro.

One of the tools used was the Organization of American States. By April 1964, Brazil closed the Cuban Embassy. That left only Chile, Uruguay, Mexico, and Bolivia with ties with Cuba.

Douglas Henderson's, the US ambassador, approach to President Paz was to point out the anomaly of Bolivia being the largest recipient of Alliance for Progress money and maintaining diplomatic relations with Cuba. Paz's response was the leftist element in Bolivia would interpret such a change as weakness on the part of the government. Henderson told Paz the large plurality with which he won the election meant he had the support of a strong majority. Paz replied it was too obvious that the OAS's action to date was based on the US position. Paz indicated there would be no change unless the OAS made it mandatory. Otherwise, it would appear he was a puppet of the U.S.

In the OAS, Bolivia voted against Cuba's intervention in Venezuela but abstained on the question of sanctions against Havana. The day after Paz's inauguration (August 6, 1964), Secretary of State Rusk cabled Ambassador Henderson that the issue of Paz's silence on Cuba was a high priority. The State Department viewed Paz's reelection as popular support for the position he had taken on receiving US Alliance for Progress aid. The State Department had not heard or not understood Paz's situation with regard to the opposition that could be mobilized by the leftist elements in Bolivia. The US position, reflected in Rusk's communique, showed a determined commitment to the isolation of Castro.

---

[77] "If you can't beat 'em, buy 'em."

On August 11, 1964, Chile voted with the U.S. in the OAS and cut diplomatic relations with Cuba. By August 13, Paz, who felt trapped in an untenable position, followed Chile's example and closed the Cuban Embassy in La Paz. That was the crucial step that triggered the unravelling of the MNR.

It was the beginning of a tumultuous time. We were not yet back two years after furlough and the country seemed like it was falling apart. Lechin, who had been the vice president in the previous administration, was replaced by General Barrientos. And, as we later learned, had not attended the inauguration because he was held incommunicado.

On September 3 a national strike of the teachers' union started and, by September 6, had quickly gained support of the miners at Siglo XX. The news came in from around the country in the following days of events there. On the sixteenth, the university students in Cochabamba sacked the USIS Center, a favorite target, destroying projectors, films, and vehicles. Beginning on the twenty-fourth, there was a form of censorship of the press with the only newspaper available in La Paz being La *Nacion* (*The Nation*)—the MNR newspaper.

There seemed little else now. As we expected, Paz announced a state of emergency throughout the whole country. It was his fifth such action since 1961. The news, mainly from the radio, was not good. The mob events were creating a state of anxiety among the foreign communities in Bolivia. Fortunately, our missionaries were holding firm and offering services as usual. Our medical facilities in some places were having rioters come in. Methodist schools were functioning, but one can imagine the environment in schools with the university students on the front lines all over. There was popular acknowledgment that October 2 was Paz's fifty-seventh birthday, but it was a half-hearted celebration.

Saddening news came on October 22. There had been two students who died from injuries sustained during riots the day before. On Friday the twenty-third, the day of the funerals, chaos broke out in every major city. Word was out that, in response, Paz had called for the mobilization of Indians and miners. This could only mean a confrontation leading to an escalation in fatalities. We didn't have to wait long. At a mock funeral held by students in Oruro over the weekend, there were four more dead.

Information was out that on Tuesday the twenty-seventh, General Barrientos met with the US air attaché in Cochabamba. The information was that Barrientos was assuring the attaché that he was the best option for a peaceful solution, and that he would be able to forestall any leftist takeover of the government. We later found out that the State Department wanted additional assurances and instructed the Bolivia desk officer, Bill Dentzer, to visit La Paz for an on the ground assessment. Dentzer left over the weekend, arriving in La Paz Sunday evening.

The situation was growing tense in La Paz. We knew truckloads of campesinos (rural Indians) and miners were arriving in the city. We limited our trips outside of the area, including only the conference office, the school grounds, and our home. There were a few missionaries who had been in the lake house who left for home. On the hillside, as was the setting of the American Institute, we had an overview of the main part of the city. The street on which the school sat was Landaeta, which emptied into the Plaza Estudientil, just a short block above San Andres University. Immediately to the left on the corner of Landaeta and the Plaza was the Ministry of Health. The next street to the left on the plaza was the municipal library wedged in, with the next being Avenida Arze or the Prado. Students pulled up the stone blocks that made the streets and formed barricades to defend the university from the government forces coming down the hill from the barracks in the center of town. Before the students retreated into the university, they firebombed the Ministry of Health and the municipal library. Meanwhile, from the institute grounds, we watched the single engine planes fly as low as possible to drop bombs (or dynamite sticks) on the students.

I had been on the plaza to watch the unfolding of all of this, but along with other spectators, I had to move back onto the campus of the school to get away from the tear gas. Over the adobe wall that separated us from the German school, we could see truckloads of men going up the street with men jumping off to break into houses in the middle-class neighborhood around the German school. We also made recordings of the sound of the planes flying low overhead, dropping bombs by hand. Monsignor Andrew

Kennedy made an appeal to the students to surrender. The paper reported that over six hundred students had been arrested.

On Monday morning Dentzer and Henderson met with President Paz. From that meeting they went to meet with General Ovando and the general staff. On Tuesday, Nov. 3 at 1:00 p.m., Paz addressed the country calling for "defense of his revolution and the economic development he had brought to the nation." Paz indicated that the "armed forces would defend public order." General Barrientos responded with a national broadcast repeating his proposal that both resign (meaning he and Paz) in favor of a military junta that would include neither Paz nor Barrientos.

On the morning of November 4, President Paz and his family fled to Lima. With the coup, the military had come full swing—from being downgraded by Paz in 1952 and the MNR revolution to ousting Paz in a military coup in 1964. We could hardly anticipate what this would mean, although we saw clearly that it would bring change and one that was far less progressive than we would have hoped for. Politically, the country had been passing through a period of grave instability. The means the military would use to attain stability would be a price paid in personal freedom. For the Methodist Church, it would mean our loss of ties to the national power structures. It was a matter of wait and see.

## 1964

## The Catholic Church in Bolivia

There were serious tensions surfacing within the Catholic Church in Bolivia. They were between the conservative hierarchy and liberal elements, primarily foreign mission orders of the church. Bolivia was not the only country where this was happening. The Vatican was aware of them and was developing a means by which to bring them to the surface and deal with them. By the late 1950s, it was ready to move. In 1962, the twenty-first ecumenical council was called into being.

The preparations for the council took three years, from the summer of 1959 to the autumn of 1962. The council opened on 11 October 1962 and concluded December 8, 1965. The council was called by Pope John XXIII because he felt the Church needed *updating* (in Italian, *aggiornamento*).

By December 1965, Vatican II, the twenty-first ecumenical council of the Roman Catholic Church, had concluded its work. The results have already been reported. What is important is how the Catholic Church in Bolivia acted out the recommendations of the council and what impact that had on Methodism.

The pressure for change and social justice in Bolivia and throughout Latin America was already developing. The Istituto Social of America Latina (ISAL), a study center in La Paz run by the Catholic Church, was producing excellent research on social conditions that many of us read with enthusiasm.[78] The Maryknoll Brothers and Sisters had been in Bolivia since about 1942. Their national center was in a suburb of Cochabamba. When we lived in Cochabamba, we frequently played volleyball with them. The order operated a language school there. In the Montero area, interchurch cooperation had expanded significantly in order to reach the needs in the colonies. However, the outcome of the council did two things: it greatly reduced the opposition and hostility Protestantism had encountered in Bolivia, and, in a short time, greatly energized Catholicism.

Maryknoll priests and sisters from the United States were soon joined by others from not only the United States but Italy and elsewhere in Europe. Laymen and laywomen joined in the mission efforts through such programs as the Papal Volunteers. In all, over thirty countries and dozens of religious communities sent missionaries to Bolivia coincided with efforts to implement reforms called for by the Second Vatican Council. The conciliar awakening among Catholics heightened the sense of responsibility of service to the poor and the native peoples and gave direction to social reform.

After Vatican II, the bishops, who had met periodically during the 1950s, formalized their gatherings. As the Bolivian Bishops' Conference, they began to exert a more active presence. They emphasized the development of basic Christian communities—the preferential option for the poor

---

[78] ISAL was later closed by the church as being too leftist in orientation.

(especially indigenous ethnic groups), lay formation programs, family life programs, and the promotion of vocations to the priesthood and religious life. The new vitality, strength, and influence were brought by the forces who felt freer in bringing social change.

In 1952, a group of lay Catholics began publishing the daily secular newspaper, *Presencia*. They gave voice to the church and competed with *La Nacion*, the paper of the MNR.

In 1966, the Catholic university was founded by the Bishops' Conference. With its center in La Paz, the school had branches in Cochabamba and Santa Cruz. The archdiocese of La Paz and the archdiocese of Santa Cruz also began campus ministry programs at state universities and teacher colleges around the country to instruct Catholic students in higher education. The giant was wakening.

The military junta in Bolivia followed up on Vatican II with an updating of the constitution. Under military rule, on Feb. 2, 1967, a new constitution was put into place in Bolivia that reflected some of these attitudes. This document recognized as official the Catholic religion and granted the church state support. Religious education was made obligatory in primary and middle schools, and the teachers received special income. It now was not a hostility to be confronted. It was an energized giant moving into areas Methodism already occupied. We would need to develop our response to these changes.

## New Missionaries in the 1960s

While it was desirable by 1965 to lower the American profile among the missionaries in Bolivia, there were jobs that could or needed to be done. Charles and Jean King came to replace Jim Palmer at Union Church, La Paz. For the first time, the board sent a team of LA 3s to Bolivia. These were recent college graduates on a short-term three-year assignments. Not only were their skills useful but their energy and enthusiasm were contagious. We welcomed a couple with skills in a new area of concern for the church, especially in the Altiplano, Herb and Darlus Schoonover.

Coming from Washington State, Herb had worked for Weyerhaeuser for some years.

> The Weyerhaeuser Company was started in 1900 by Frederick Weyerhaeuser as a timber company. Today it owns over 11 million acres of timberland in the U.S. It collaborates through contracts in the management of millions of acres of public land in Canada. It operates under a plan of sustainability and renewal.

The Schoonovers were another couple who came to us from Chile, as did the Barbers and the Fritzs.

The diversity was growing within the membership. Ethnic or tribal background played an important role in Bolivia. The tensions of society were beginning to be felt within Methodism. The demographic change in membership was desirable but would be stressful. It was increasingly clear that we would need to be more direct in dealing with these new developments. In conversations with the Board of Missions, one of the possibilities was to develop a better understanding of points of view and issues of concern. The board indicated its willingness to find someone from the field of anthropology or sociology who could assist the conference leadership in understanding some of the issues involved.

In 1965, a formal request was made to the board to send an anthropologist to assist us to understand and accommodate the diversity of. John and Carolyn Hickman arrived in 1966.

Along with ethnic tensions, illiteracy continued to be a serious problem. Bolivian Methodism had become involved with ALFALIT, a program to teach illiterates to read throughout the country already referred to at length. But by the 1960s, we began to hear about a new methodology of teaching literacy to the poor being used in Brazil. Jim Pace was aware of it and brought it to the attention of several others of us. It was a form of consciousness-raising through teaching literacy. The source of the information was Dr. Richard Shaull, professor at the Presbyterian seminary in Brazil who was disseminating information about the methodology.

In 1965, Paulo Freire was in Bolivia for a short period of time before continuing on to Chile. In 1968, his second book came off the press and was like a bombshell, *Pedagogy of the Oppressed* in Spanish. The English version was available in 1970. In that year, Freire was invited to join the staff of the World Council of Churches as a special educational advisor where he worked for the next ten years. Freire was born in Recife, Brazil, in 1921; one of the most extreme examples of urban poverty. The Great Depression hit the U.S, and then most of world. Freire's middle-class family soon was among the *wretched of the world*. Freire saw the educational system as one of the instruments for the maintenance of the *culture of silence*. His dissertation at the University of Recife was his first articulation of using teaching literacy as the means of radicalization. It was obvious that Freire's methodology was relevant to conditions in Bolivia.

Richard Shaull graduated from seminary in 1941. As serving a year as a parish minister in Texas, he applied to the Board of Missions. After a term in Brazil, he returned to seminary to train to be a seminary professor in Campinas, Brazil. But his theology was shaped by his experience of the oppression of the poor. Shaull had a keen sense of justice he applied to social conditions around him. He interpreted what he saw through the lens of a profound faith.

It was difficult to know how effective the Friere teaching method would be, but the impact at its introduction was quite significant. It seemed to bring together the feelings for social justice with the desire to learn as never experienced before. It is worth sharing Friere's background to understand his importance better.

Paulo Freire was born on September 19, 1921, to a middle-class family in Recife, the capital of the northeastern Brazilian state of Pernambuco. He became familiar with poverty and hunger from an early age as a result of the Great Depression.

During his childhood and adolescence, Freire ended up four grades behind. Freire stated that poverty and hunger severely affected his ability to learn. These experiences influenced his decision to dedicate his life to improving the lives of the poor: "I didn't understand anything because of my hunger.

I wasn't dumb. It wasn't lack of interest. Experience showed me once again the relationship between social class and knowledge."

Freire enrolled in law school at the University of Recife in 1943. He also studied philosophy, more specifically phenomenology, and the psychology of language. Although admitted to the legal bar, he never practiced law and instead worked as a secondary school Portuguese teacher.

In 1946, Freire began to develop an educational theory that would have an influence on the liberation theology movement of the 1970s. In the1940s, literacy was a requirement for voting in presidential elections in Brazil.

In 1962, as director of an extension program for the university, in an experiment, three hundred sugarcane harvesters were taught to read and write in just forty-five days. But the 1964 military coup put an end to Freire's literacy effort. After a brief exile in Bolivia, Freire worked in Chile for five years for the Christian Democratic Agrarian Reform Movement and the United Nations Food and Agriculture Organization.

In 1967, Freire published his first book, *Education as the Practice of Freedom*. He followed it up with his most famous work, *Pedagogy of the Oppressed*, which was first published in 1968.

Friere's educational theory, combined with the theology of liberation, was the source of the energy driving the revitalization of Catholicism. But it never would have happened without Vatican II.

## Che Guevara in Bolivia

Che Guevara arrived in Bolivia in November 1966. He came for the purpose of not just supporting a communist takeover of the government of Bolivia, but to set up a secure base for communist activity in all of South America. Ernest Guevara was born in Rosario, Argentina, on June 14, 1928. Che made several trips around Latin America, including one on an unreliable Norton motorcycle with Alberto Granado in 1952. His journal of the trip was turned into the book, *Motorcycle Diaries*. He was already actually living in Guatemala in 1952 when the duly elected government of Arbenz was overthrown in a CIA-organized military operation. Che made his escape to Mexico, profoundly radicalized by what he had gone through. In Mexico, he sought out contact with a group of Cubans who were in exile from the Fulgencio Batista regime in Cuba. On November 25, 1956, Guevara set sail for Cuba on the yacht, *Granma*. Guevara, serving as medical doctor to the Cuban guerrillas, was joining the band in the Sierra Maestra Mountains where he met Castro. Some months later, Che was named by Fidel to head the first rebel army. Following the collapse of the Batista government in January 1959, Che became a key leader in the revolutionary government holding several important positions.

Che Guevara left Cuba in April 1965 for the Congo, Africa, to support a revolutionary movement. He returned to Cuba by December 1965 to prepare for a similar trip to Bolivia. Che's diary was recovered so we have Che's perspective on the final days of his life. The last entry is on October 7, 1966. He died of wounds on October 8, 1966.

The months before his death, we (Methodists) were aware of development from another perspective. The national radio net of the Methodists, which was created and maintained by Loyde Middleton by using surplus US radios from Air Force bombers, was on the *horn* at 6:00 a.m. and again at 6:00 p.m. Whenever possible, I was at the room in the boy's dorm at the American Institute which served as the radio *shack* in La Paz. News from pastors made me aware of new families in our congregations. Some of these new visitors attended service in English at one of the Union Churches. Other reports came from pastors of Spanish congregations and of visitors who spoke with a Cuban or Central American accent. I also received news of unusual movement of Bolivian troops with American advisors. There were rumors that a companion of Che's group named Tania had some dubious relationship with the American Institute.[79]

---

[79] The story pf Tania, an Argentinian by birth, gives insight into the training of undercover foreign agents. Tania was given the cover of specialist in folklore and ethnography. She was to be located in La Paz in order to develop special contacts with government officials, the bourgeoisie, and the military forces. She quickly integrated herself into these groups. Tania was killed on August 31, 1967. Che died October 8, 1967. See for details, Estrada's *Tania*.

The incident ended the Cuban military adventurism in Latin America, but was one of the several elements in which the US government was involved in its confrontation with communism in this hemisphere.

I would classify it as a major unfortunate, unavoidable affair. Not because it was Cuba or because it was a failure, it was tragic because it brought the United States more directly than before into the affairs of Bolivia. The covert activity undertaken by the U.S only fed the flames of anti-US-ism that already existed. The US action was not different than on several other prior occasions. What was different was that Barrientos was president, not Paz. President Paz had a way of working with the US adventurism. Barrientos was now the president. And Barrientos was a general who made coups the acceptable means to change governments. He created his own problem, now he must contend with the ambitions of other generals who have his precedent as their example.

## The McCleary Family

As we began looking forward to the end of our second term in Bolivia, our children were coming to the age when the older two were planning for college. We were going home at the end of 1968. Leslie Ann would be in her senior year of high school. Rachel Mary would be in her sophomore year. Rachel was becoming a little concerned about their futures. We both wanted the children to attend college as we had. The girls themselves would have to answer where they would like to attend and what they would like to study.

Since moving to La Paz in 1963, all four of the children were enrolled in the American Institute. This meant they were studying in a Spanish environment. The concern was to be sure they would be able to gain entrance to a college on the basis of seeking entrance with an international educational background. A second concern was that the girls would be ready for being in an American college. We were hearing about so much happening on campuses with the anti-Vietnam war movement and the drug culture. They would be encountering a great for which they had not been prepared.

Maxima, Rachel Mary, Leslie Ann Valentine,
John Wesley, and Timothy Paul

Leslie graduated from grade school at the American Institute in 1963, and continued on in high school there through the 1965 school year. We decided it best for her to finish high school at the cooperative school, a grade and high school that was based on the Calvert correspondence system licensed in the State of Virginia. The school was taught in English and located in Calacoto, a wealthy suburban of La Paz where many Americans lived. As time grew closer for her to decide, she applied to and was accepted at Florida Southern College, a Methodist College in Lakeland, Florida. I think her choice was Lakeland because it was on our path back and forth to Illinois, and she hoped we might see her more frequently on future trips to Bolivia or home. Rachel and I readily agreed. Florida Southern College is a small college with a beautiful campus around Lake Hollingsworth, with buildings designed by Frank Lloyd Wright.

Rachel Mary, two years younger than Leslie, attended the Calvert Cooperative School for her first year of high school. She was elected secretary of the student government and played on the basketball team. After conversations with my brother, Rachel Mary returned with Lloyd to Champaign-Urbana, Illinois, to start her sophomore year at Centennial High School. On our return to the States, we moved to Englewood Cliffs, New Jersey, where Mary completed her sophomore year, and Leslie graduated from Dwight Morrow High School. We then moved to Glenview, Illinois. Mary attended Glenbrook South High School. Elected vice president of the school's student body, Rachel Mary also served as editor of the literary magazine. One afternoon in January 1970, Rachel called the principal's office at the high school asked us for a meeting. As you can imagine, my mind began to spin about what the issue could be for such urgency.

Beginning in 1970, a number of states, including Illinois, sought to make Martin Luther King's birthday, January 15, a holiday. Our daughter was one in a group of students leading a sit-in in the principal's office over the speaker for Martin Luther King Day—not yet a federal holiday. At local levels, municipalities, like Chicago, and states celebrated his holiday, and Illinois became the first state in 1973 to officially recognize Martin Luther King Day. The principal of Glenbrook South High School thought he could resolve the matter by asking the pastor of First United Methodist Church, Glenview to be the speaker. Our daughter, among others, was continuing the sit-in because they wanted a black to speak. I could only say that it seemed like a reasonable request. Mary chose to attend the University of Denver, an institution with Methodist origins. She continued her studies, earning a doctorate from the University of Chicago.

Our third child, John Wesley, was destined to follow the course of action of his sisters to a point. As a student at the American Institute, he had many friends. There were several other missionary children in grade school. One of the families that lived on campus was Gary and Mary Fritz. Among their several children was Gary Nathan, who was one of John's good friends. The Fritzs had several pets for their children, one of which was a llama. They boys had a great time trying to ride him. Another close friend of his was Mark Barber. The Barbers lives in Obrajes near the hospital and school of nursing. John and Mark had the run of the hospital.

One of their pastimes was to explore the Methodist Hospital where Ed Barber served as chaplain. They discovered, by laying on their stomachs on the roof, they could look down through the skylight of the operating room to watch the surgery going on. That little escapade ended when one of the patients had a local anesthesia and laid on the operating table looking up to see two small boys looking down at him.

Another good friend of John's was Jimmy Pace. The Paces lived in Montero, some distance from La Paz, but Jimmy's friendship grew stronger after we left Bolivia. Jimmy spent a few days with us before his trip to Europe some years later. John was of an age that during school vacations I could take him with me on trips that allowed some time free for him. He has some interesting stories to tell about trips to Eastern Bolivia. Reference has already been made to one of the trips. Another story he enjoys telling is about a visit we made to the Beni in the rainy season. Most of our travel that trip had to be on horseback since much of the land was covered by almost a foot of water. He hadn't expected he would have the thrill of horseback riding for several days.

Our youngest child is Timothy Paul, six years younger than John. Tim wrote this about memory of school in Bolivia:

> I was in the American Institute for at least one year. I rode in the passenger seat of the Volkswagen van. The driver would share his snacks with me, some kind of a small nut. John waited (on the street corner) with me until I was picked up. One time there was a Halloween party of sorts and us kindergarteners were taken outside to see the students parade around the center courtyard in their costumes. John was dressed as a football player, and the teacher told me, "There's your brother!" I didn't recognize him. I asked where my sisters were, and she said they were in the upper grades (high school).

Tim also wrote about one of the trips to the Altiplano on which he accompanied me:

> I also remember riding with you to the Altiplano before I started school, and you made the car purposely slow down

going uphill and fast on the other side. When we got to the opening of a new clinic, the doctor and nurses helped with pulling an infected tooth of a Native person, who was on a gurney, as an example of possible services.

It frequently occurred that a person would wait too long for medical attention. It made quite an impression on my five-year-old the difficulty they had in extracting an infected tooth. Tim went on to earn a doctorate at the University of Illinois in Champaign-Urbana.

Missionary children are exposed to a world of differences from other children. Like every child, it is important how they understand what is happening around them, and how to respond appropriately so they are equipped for what they will experience in life on their own.

There are two people who became part of our family when we lived in La Paz. One of these was Maxima Catacorra de Pajaro. She was our maid. That has special meaning in Bolivia. There was a washing machine that worked on its own schedule. Too often clothes were handwashed. There was no electric dryer. Clothes were hung out to dry. The cost of canned goods or cereals, when available, was beyond our budget. Weekly, there were several trips to the market or a neighborhood store. Usually, the maid lived in. That was not the case with Maxima. She could travel home on evenings to her family. During the day, she cared for our children as if they were her own. She was an immense help around the house. Maxima became a close companion to Rachel.

The maid's quarters were occupied by a young man from one of our schools on the Altiplano. Valentino Anahuaya was a gifted young man who deserved an opportunity to continue his education. Valentino lived with us and attended the American Institute. John took an interest in Valentino, and they became good companions.

The major pull of the United States was the desire to see grandparents. Their attachments in Bolivia were going to be hard to overcome. Just how strong the pull of Bolivia would be on their lives came soon after we settled in New Jersey.

I was asked to work at the Board of Missions in New York. We found a place to live in Englewood Cliffs, New Jersey. The children were all enrolled in the appropriate schools. It wasn't long after we have settled into the schedule of work and school that John brought home a message that his teacher would like a parent-teacher conference about John's work. Together, Rachel and I met with John's teacher. She explained as diplomatically as possible that she believed that John had a learning disability. He wasn't measuring up to others in his grade, and he seemed to not be taking his assignments seriously. She would like to recommend, she said, that he visit the school psychologist to get a better understanding of what his problems might be.

We could hardly believe what she was implying. At the same time, we, too, wanted to know if there was a problem that needed attention. We agreed. We indicated to John what was going to happen. We explained that it was a matter of a conversation and perhaps a few simple tests.

With a degree of anxiety and anticipation, we waited for a conference with the school psychologist and John's teacher. The psychologist began the conversation with a few words to acknowledge that she was aware that we had been living overseas. She noted that it meant there was a matter of adjustment to a new environment involved for all of us. We waited anxiously for what she was leading up to. So we were surprised when she said, "John's problem is he doesn't think this is home. He is coasting in his work, waiting for you to go home to Bolivia."

She recommended that we take time to clarify with John what our intentions were. She had made us aware that our children were getting to the age when they needed to become a part of the decision-making we did as we moved forward with our lives together.

# Chapter IX

## 1968

After conference closed in November 1967, reality began to set in. This was our last year before our furlough in the United States. This meant that whatever needed to be done, I would need to start soon to accomplish it. It also meant that I needed to come to the realization that some things just would have to be finished by others.

Several matters had been set in motion at conference about things that needed to be done to qualify for the status of an autonomous church. These included the preparation of a constitution, a book of discipline for church order, and necessary communications to various persons and entities in order that the appropriate action be taken at the general conference in 1968. It would be useful also to be in constant touch with the other conferences in the Latin American Central Conference to be sure of their determinations concerning autonomy. This would be a priority concern throughout the year.

The bishops' appointments have been made with prayerful consideration to match abilities and skills with current needs and challenges. Every year here in Bolivia, I felt that the level of professional skills had increased. There could hardly be put together a finer group of skilled and dedicated individuals. I have felt a profound sense of honor to be among such a fine group of persons working together to produce the best outcomes possible. I am sure Bishop Barbieri felt the same way. As we bid goodbye, I sensed he felt relaxed and satisfied with what had been done at the conference. I recalled his impassioned presentation at Garrett years before, and now how far Methodism had come in fulfilling a commitment to the indigenous communities in Bolivia.

The major ongoing concern had been to assure the financial support for the social work of Methodism beyond its congregations. The continuing support from Oklahoma and Texas had remained strong. The possible dip was gradual, not as great as I had anticipated. Regarding income generation from Bolivian sources, the major project—the COSMOS building—was well under construction, but a loan was still under negotiation to assure the completion of the construction.

Local funding for church and schools was growing. In the field of education, the number of schools had grown considerably. This was especially so on the Altiplano, in the Yungas, the Chapare, and Santa Cruz areas. The government establishment of new schools had not kept pace with the population growth and migrations. The establishment of a school seemed to go hand in hand with establishing a congregation. The emphasis on improving the quality of the education being provided was also having its impact.

Methodist educators, such as Gaston Pol, were having an influence beyond Methodism.

The training of church workers had come a long way from the days when we sent young men to seminary in Buenos Aires. The programs to train church workers in Ancoraimes and Montero placed their education in a context more typical to where they would serve. New personnel arrived to strengthen the outreach, such as the Ernie and Anita Eppley, Carl and Julia Williams, and Herb and Darlus Schoonover.

The education work was significantly strengthened through the two institutes, as well as the internado in Sucre by new personnel arriving: Bill Frank John and Wanda Schmidt, David and Carol Adams, Adele Phillips, Dale and Judy Good, Russell and Cecilia Dilley, David and Carole Adams, Richard and Lila Palmiter, Eloise Beadles, and Jim Tuttle. Montero work benefited by new personnel for it agriculture and vocational training program. Wendall and Ruth Kramer came from a background in managing a cooperative farm program. The Kramer sons, Loren, was gifted in weaving and textiles, while Stanley in agriculture. Other new personnel assigned to one of the programs based in Montero included Harry and Pat Peacock, Ann Love, Barbara Caufield, and a number of LA 3s to work at the school and in the colonies.

The medical work had come such a long way since Dr. Beck. It had gone to the frontiers of Methodism, along with education. Extensive reference has already been made about the medical expansion with the presence of Pablo Monti, Enrique Cicchetti, and Saturnino Guicheney. Methodism's commitment to the whole person—soul, mind, and body—was visibly expressed by the nature of its presence in church, school, and medical clinic together. This vision had been drummed into all of us by being the motto of the American Institutes.

The work of ethnolinguistic Aymara in urban areas, as well as on the Altiplano, was growing at almost an exponential rate. It was not only through the compesinos (farmer) elements as a heritage of persons such as Felipe Flores, or Daniel Marconi, the small commercial element, it was growing among future teachers and others receiving an education at Warisata through work begun by Dobinson and Mary Catherine McAden.

There was a nagging thought that haunted me. It was that Methodism would have to think about ceasing to do some things. It is hard to move on to be something else unless you give up some of what you were. I did not feel it was my responsibility to begin that process, but it would come.

## Fourth Assembly of the WCC

In early spring of 1968, an invitation came from the World Council of Churches to send a visitor to the fourth assembly in Uppsala, Sweden, in July. The invitation was, obviously, extended to the conference due to the forthcoming autonomy. The executive committee of the conference proposed I should be the representative to attend. Bishop Barbieri was concluding his term as one of the presidents of the WCC. It would be an honor to be present.

Upon exploring travel plans, I discovered the round trip ticket allowed several stopovers both going and returning. The trip provided an unusual opportunity to make visits to colleagues in several other countries, especially in Europe.

One of the scheduled speakers was Dr. Martin Luther King who had just been assassinated in Memphis. The world was experiencing ferment in several quarters. The Prague Spring uprising had occurred. University students were rioting in Paris. Peace marches were taking place all over the U.S., increasing commitment to a war in Vietnam. South Africa was in the throes of anti-apartheid violence. The Cold War continued to divide the world. Excitement grew as the thought of what it would mean to attend a meeting of the World Council of Churches where delegates from all over the world would be present.

Once I had registered, I began to grasp the magnitude of what it would mean to attend. There were over two thousand participants of which 702 were delegates from 225 member churches in over eighty countries. To report the assembly, there were over seven hundred accredited journalists. To assist with the day-to-day work, there were over three hundred stewards.

Uppsala, the site of the Assembly, was one of historic grandeur. The city was the *church capital* for the country for over eight hundred years, with a cathedral built in 1415. Uppsala University, begun in 1477, would rank as the *Harvard* of Sweden.

In light of world events, the theme for the assembly was a very appropriate one, "Behold, I make all things new." Global Christianity itself was being *made new*. The Second Vatican held in 1962–65, which brought refreshing breezes of change to Catholicism, was present with an active fifteen-person observer delegation. The Orthodox churches were very active participants in the sessions of the plenary. There were, for the first time, one hundred and fifty youth participants with equal representation from all continents. A transforming dimension of the assembly was the communications revolution, which had taken place since the last assembly. The major events of the assembly were Sweden's first successful international color TV event. The assembly was planned to be as transparent as possible. Daily news of the assembly was reaching every corner of the world. The news not only was the assembly itself through the daily briefings but included the news protests taking place outside it.

In the land of eternal sunrise, the days became much longer. One of the aspects I personally enjoyed was to drop in at one of the evening coffeehouses. It was always an unusual gathering of youth and older church leaders who came to enjoy the music, dance, and entertainment, such as folk singer Pete Seeger.

A major issue of the assembly was racism. Martin Luther King was replaced by the novelist James Baldwin. The assembly considered such situations as apartheid in Southern Africa, and established a new action program—the WCC's Program to Combat Racism. In response to the new ecumenism, nine Roman Catholic theologians were added to the Faith and Order Commission. One of the key speakers was Dr. Barbara Ward, a Roman Catholic and famous British economist who spoke convincingly about world poverty and global trade issues.

One of the fallouts of attendance at the assembly was that in planning for the transitional Annual Conference sessions in Bolivia, the theme chosen for the conference was, "Behold, I make all things new."[80]

In September 1968, Dr. Lloyd McCleary came to complete the program he had laid out for teacher training. When he returned to the U.S., Rachel Mary accompanied him to complete her high school education in the U.S. and prepare her for college. The other three shifted from the American Institute to the Calvert or Cooperative School to be in an English program for a transition to schools in the U.S.

## The 1968 Annual Conference Sessions

In planning for the sessions of the Annual Conference, I could not help but think back to the 1961 sessions when I succeeded Murray. The accidental death of Murray and Lou hung heavy over the conference. We had picked

---

[80] See the official report of the Fourth Assembly of the World Council of Churches, Uppsala, Sweden, July 3–20, 1968.

up on the planning, much of which was in Murray's mind. Good progress had been made on all fronts of the life of the church, but the grief from our losses could not be dispelled. The church was a family. We had lost two important members of our small community. It was a relief when the conference ended.

As we moved into the actual activities of the 1968 conference sessions, the mood was quite different than that of the first conference at which I was executive secretary in 1961. Significant progress had been made on all fronts for the church. Congregational life was now at a point of significant takeoff. Financial support from sources other than the congregations was well on the way to be a reality with the COSMOS building under construction and the Icthus Press being launched. An important part of the positive mood of the participants was in the expectation of a new form in the immediate future with the granting of autonomy by the General Conference in 1968.

Mario Salazar, Bishop Barbieri, President Rene Barrientos, Angel Balcivieso, and Gaston Pol, 1968 Annual Conference, Cochabamba, Bolivia. Awarding of the Condor of the Andes to Bishop Barbieri.

As a symbol of that transition, the Annual Conference wanted to acknowledge the visionary leadership which Bishop Barbieri had provided to bringing the Bolivian church to maturity. On hand to bestow this honor was Rene Barrientos, President of Bolivia, along with his Minister of Education, Angel Balcivieso. The medal, the Condor of the Andes, was awarded to Bishop Barbieri. The first Methodist to receive such award honored Dr. Frank Beck. The Condor of the Andes is the highest nonmilitary award the Bolivian government can give.

National public recognition of Methodism went beyond the honor Bishop Barbieri received, since Dr. Gaston Pol had been recently named to the President's Committee on Education for Bolivia.

The conference sessions closed with the traditional reading of appointments and the sharing of the sacrament of the Lord's Supper. There was a celebratory mood of enthusiasm and optimism as the delegates and visitors greeted each other with best wishes and a warm abrazo (hug).

With the conference sessions ended, Rachel and I could finally relax. It was time to think about our personal future. The Board of Missions had asked if I would join the staff in New York and assist in the implementation of the new quadrennial emphasis approved by the 1968 General Conference. We accepted that challenge as the means to allow time to examine what the future might hold for us. Regardless of what that might be, we knew our future would forever be shaped by our having been to Bolivia.

# BIBLIOGRAPHY

Aguilar, Raquel Gutierrez. *Rhythms of the Pachatuti: Indigenous Uprising and the State Power in Bolivia.* Durham and London: Duke University Press, 2014.

Alexander. *The Bolivian National Revolution.* New Brunswick, NJ: Rutgers University Press, 1958.

Barber, Natalie. *Passport to Faith.* Arizona: Self-published, 2003.

Beck, Bessie. *History of the Medical Work of The United Methodist Church in Bolivia.* Unpublished document, 85 pp. Library of Margaret Dickson, 1974.

Besk, Bessie. *A Study of Changing Social Attitudes in the American Institutes of Bolivia.* A part of a dissertation submitted to the faculty of the Divinity School for the degree of Doctor of Philosophy1935. Chicago, Illinois: distributed by the University of Chicago Libraries, 1938.

Boots, Wilson T. *Protestant Christianity in Bolivia Mission Theory and Practice in Three Mission Churches.* Washington, D.C.: The American University, 1971.

Buechler, Hans. *The Bolivian Aymara.* Holt, Rinehart and Winslow, Inc., 1971.

Burns, Ray G. *The American Institute of la Paz, Bolivia, A Study of Its Influence for Social Progress.* Unpublished dissertation for Master of Arts degree to Department of History Oklahoma Agricultural and Mechanical College, 1838.

Cohen, Alvin. *Bolivia: Internal Instability and International Dependence, During the Period 1961-1969, Bolivia's Development Process was Characterized by Her Dependence on Her Foreign Sector for Financing Capital Accumulation, Current History.* Feb. 1, 1971.

Copplestone, Tremayne. *Twentieth-Century Perspectives (the Methodist Episcopal Church, 1896–1939) - History of Methodist Missions Volume IV.* New York: GBGM Book, 1973.

Cote, Stephen. *Oil and Nation A History of Bolivia's Petroleum Sector.* Morgantown, WV: West Virginia University Press, 2016.

Craine, E.J. *Airline Boys with the Revolutionaries in Bolivia.* PUP Press, University of Purdue Press, 1003 (Original printing in 1931).

Dangl, Benjamin. *The Five Hundred Year Rebellion Indigenous Movements and the Decolonization of History in Bolivia.* Chico. California: AK Press, 2019.

Dangl, Benjamin. *The Price of Fire: Resource Wars and Social Movements in Bolivia.* Oakland, California: AK Press, 2007.

Dickson, Murray Barbieri, Sante U. *Bolivia Conference correspondence.* Unpublished, 1957–1961.

Private collection of Margaret Dickson.

Dickson, Murray. *Latin American Youth in a World of Ferment.* Buck Hill Falls, Pennsylvania: presented to the Study Conference of the Committee on Cooperation in Latin America, November 1960, 16 pp.

Estrada, Ulises. *Tania, Undercover with Che Guevara in Bolivia.* New York: Ocean Press, 2005.

Farah, David. *Bolivia: Silent Partner in the Bolivarian Joint Criminal Enterprise Evo Morales.* Miami, FL: International Institute for Democracy, Fon do Editorial, 2019.

Farthing, Linda. *Coup A Story of Violence and Resistance in Bolivia.* Chicago, Illinois: Haymarket Books, 2021.

Farthing, Linda. *Evo's Bolivia Community and Change.* Austin: University of Texas Press, 2014.

Field, James C. *From Development to Dictatorship Bolivia and the Alliance for Progress.* Ithaca, NY: Cornell University Press, 2014.

Field, Thomas C. "Union Busting as Development: Transnationalism, Empire and Kennedy's Secret Labor Programme for Bolivia." Journal of Latin American Studies 2020, 52 (September 10, 2019): 27–51.

Goldner, Laren. "Anti-Capitalism or Anti-Imperialism? Interwar Authoritarian and Fascist Sources of a Reactionary Ideology: The Case of the Bolivian MNR" Journal of Communist Theory and Practice, vol #3 (December 2010): p. 104.

Guevara, Ernesto Che. *The Bolivian Diary.* New York: Ocean Press, 2006.

Gustafson, Bret. *Bolivia in An Age of Gas.* Durham, NC: Duke University Press, 2020.

Harmon, Robert J. *From Missions to Mission the History of Mission of the United Methodist Church 1908-2000.* GBGM Books, 2000.

Hartell, Floy Collins. *A Monument of Faith The Story of 28 Years in the Mission Field.* Unpublished copy compiled from the Rev. Frank and Laura Hartzell, 1906–1934.

Hawkes, J.G. *The Potato, Evolution, Biodiversity and Genetic Resource.* London: The University of Nottingham Trent Press, 1980.

Historical Society. *La Iglesia Metodista en Bolivia 1906-1961 The Methodist Church in Bolivia 1906-1961.* Authorized by the Annual Conference, published. The Historical Society, 1961.

Johansson, Goran. *More Blessed to Give A Pentecostal Mission to Bolivia in Anthropological Perspective.* Department of Social Studies, Stockholm, Sweden Stockholm University, 1992

Kimball, Natalie. *An Open Secret The History of Unwanted Pregnancies and Abortion in Modern Bolivia.* New Brunswick, New Jersey: Rutgers University Press.

Lehman, Kenneth D. *Bolivia and the United States.* Athens, GA: University of Georgia Press, 1999.

Lehman, Kenneth D. "Completing the Revolution? The United States and Bolivia's Long Revolution." Bolivian Studies Journal Vol. 22 (2016).

Luykx. *The Citizen Factory, Schooling and Cultural Production in Bolivia.*

Malloy, James M. and Gomarra, Eduardo. *La Transicion a la Democracia en Bolivia.*

Malloy, James and Gamarra, Eduardo. *Revolution and Reaction: Bolivia 1964–1985.* New Brunswick, New Jersey: Transaction Inc., 1988.

Malloy, James and Richard Thorn. *Beyond the Revolution Bolivia Since 1952.* Pittsburgh, PA: University of Pittsburgh Press, 1971.

Mamani, Pasqual Luque. *Historia de la Iglesia Metodista en Bolivia, en el Primer Centenario 1906–2006.* El Alto de La Paz: Coordinacion de Impresion CEBIAE, 2006.

McFarren, Peter and Fadriquo, Iglesias. *The Devil's Agent: Life, Times and Crimes of Nazi Klaus Barbie.* Indianapolis: Xlibris, 2013.

Mora, Mariana. *Kuxlejal Politics: Indigenous Autonomy, Race, and Decolonizing Research in Zapatista Communities.* Austin: University of Texas, 2017.

Niebuhr, Robert. *Vamos A Avanzar! The Chaco War and Bolivia's Political Transformation, 1899–1952*. Lincoln, Nebraska: University of Nebraska, 2021.

Oglesby, Carl and Shaull, Richard. *Containment and Change Two dissenting Views of American Foreign Policy*. New York: MacMillan Company, 1967.

Pace III, James W. *Mother of Exiles Interviews on Asylum Seekers*. St. Louis: Angelus Artists Productions Inc., 2022.

Pacino, Nicole. "Bringing the Revolution to the Countryside Rural Health Programmes as State Building in Post-1952 Bolivia." *Bulletin of Latin American Research, Journal of the Society for Latin American Studies* Vol. 38, No. 1 (2019) 50–65.

Payne, Will and Wilson, Charles T.W. *Missionary Pioneering in Bolivia, with Some Account of Work in Argentina*. Paternoster Square, London: published by H.A. Raymond, 1900.

Palmer, James B. *Red Poncho and Big Boots, The Life of Murray Dickson*. Nashville: Patheon Press, 1969; 1984.

Paul, T. V., Wirtz, James J., and Fortmann, Michael. *Balance of Power Theory and Practice in the 21$^{st}$ Century*. Stanford, California: Stanford University Pres, 2004.

Peacock, Patricia Corbello and Bell, Jane Collins. *We Chose Bolivia, An Intimate Memoir About the Struggles of a Missionary Family in a Land of Great Promise and Dire Problems*. 817 Jennifer Court, Sanger, Texas 76266: self-published, 2009. Poma, Eugenio and James B. Palmer, Sr. *Journey To Dignity the Autobiography of Bishop Eugenio Poma Anaguaya*. Alton, Texas: Timberwolf Press, 2006.

Porterfield, Bruce C. *Commandos for Christ the Gospel Witness in Bolivia. The Gospel Witness in Bolivia's Green Hell*. New York: Harper and Row, 1964.

Postero, Nancy. *The Indigenous State Race, Politics, and Performance in Plurinational Bolivia*. Oakland, California: University of California Press, 2017.

Quispe, Delfin E. *Historia de la Iglesia Metodista en Bolivia Una Iglesia Evangelica Inculturado, 1906–2006*. La Paz, Bolivia: Ediciones Graficas VIRTUAL, 2006.

Read, William R. Monterroso, Victor M., and Johnson, H A. *Latin American Church Growth*. Grand Rapids, Michigan: Wm Eerdmans Publishing Co., 1969.

Rejas Heredia, Evelyn, *Sociedad, Politica y Crisis Social En Bolivia*. Editorial Academica Espanola, 2012.

Shesko, Elizabeth. *Conscript Nation Coercion and Citizenship in the Bolivian Barracks*. Pittsburgh, PA: University of Pittsburgh Press, 2020.

Smith, Eugene, Barbieri, Sante U., Booth, Newell, Brewster, Harold, Brumbaugh, Thoburn, and Pickett, Waskom. *Lands of witness and Decision*. New York: Board of Missions of the Methodist Church, 1957.

Smith, Eugene, Barbieri, Sante U., Booth, Newell, Brewster, Harold, Brumbaugh, Thoburn, and Pickett, Waskom, *Lands of witness and Decision*. New York: Board of Missions of the Methodist Church, 1957.

Soliz, Carmen. *Fields of Revolution Agrarian Reform and Rural State Formation in Bolivia 1953–1964*. Pittsburgh, Pennsylvania: University of Pittsburgh Press, 2021.

Stillwell, H.L. *Pioneering in Bolivia*, The Canadian Baptist Foreign Mission Board, Toronto, Canada, ca 1924, pp. 243,

Thiessen, Ben Nobbs. *Landscape of Migration: Mobility and Environmental Change in Bolivia's Tropical Frontier 1952 to the Present*. Chapel Hill: University of North Carolina Press, 2020.

US Government. *Point Four in Bolivia, 1942–1960, Program of Technical Cooperation and Economic Assistance of the United States of America and Bolivia*.

Warren, Leslie F. *The Land and People of Bolivia (Portraits of the Nations Series, Volume 8)*. New York: J.B. Lippencott Company, 1974.

Webber, Jeffery. *From Rebellion to Reform in Bolivia, Class Struggle, Indigenous Liberation, and the Politics of Evo Morales*. Chicago, Illinois: Haymarket Books, 2011.

Young, Kevin A. *Blood on the Earth Resource Nationalism, Revolution, and Empire in Bolivia*. Austin: University of Texas Press, 2017.

Young, Kevin A. *From Open Door to Nationalization: Oil and Development Visions in Bolivia, 1962–1969*. Harvard University: Duke Press, 1997.

Young. Kevin A. *Restoring Discipline to the Ranks the United States and the Restructuring of the Bolivian Mining Industry 1960-1970, Latin American Perspectives* Issue 179, Vol. 38, no. 6 (Nov. 2011).

Zulawski, Ann. *Unique Cures Public Health and Political Change in Bolivia, 1900–1950*. Durham, NC: Duke University Press, 2007.

## Nazism in Bolivia

Calderon, Fernando. "Diez Tesis Sobre el Conflicto Social in America Latina." *Revista CEPAL* (Agosto 2012): 7–29.

Fagone, Jason. *The Woman Who Smashed Codes A True Story pf Love, Spies, and the Unlikely Heroine Who Outwitted America's Enemies*. New York Harper Collins, 2017.

Hancock, Eleanor. *Ernst Rohm: Hitler's S. A. Chief of Staff*. Palgrave/MacMillan Reprint, 2011.

Hancock, Eleanor. "Ernst Rohm Versus General Hans Kundt in Bolivia 1929–1930? The Curious Incident Journal of Contemporary History." *University of New South Wales, Australia*.

Lorini, Irma. *Nazis in Bolivia: Its Militants and Supporters 1929–1945*. La Paz: Plural Editores,[81] 2016.

---

[81] Plural Ediyores is an editorial in Bolivia with a network of bookstores across the country. It is both publisher and seller. It advertises in Facebook.

Hall, Melvin. "Wings fir the Trojan Horse." *Foreign Affairs, Vol. 19, No. #2* (Story of Lloyd Aereo Boliviano Airlines, other foreign owned airlines in LA) (January 1941): 347–369.

Mowry, David P. *Cryptologic Aspects of German Intelligence Activities in South America During World War II*. Center for Cryptologic History, National Security Agency, 2011.

Mowry, David P. *Operation Bolivar Establishment and Operation of Clandestine Communications Between Latin America and Europe*. Center for Cryptologic History, National Security Agency, 2013.

Porter, Russell. "Nazis Forming Fifth Column in Bolivia to Wrest Tin Industry From U.S. If Germany Wins War," *The Washington Post*, July 28, 1940.

Spitzer, Leo. "Persistent memory: Central European Refugees in an Andean Land." *ISTOR* Vol. 17, #4 published by Duke University Press (Winter of 1996): 617–638 (22).

Spitzer, Leo. "Rootless Diaspora: Vienna in La Paz, La Paz in Elsewhere." *Special Edition: The Jewish Diaspora*, Shofar, Vol, 19, No. #3 published by Purdue University Press (Spring, 2001): 6–17.

Stahl, Daniel. *Hunt for Nazis: South America's Dictatorships and the Protection of Nazi Crimes*. Amsterdam University Press, 2018.

## Documents File

Boots, Wilson T., unpublished documents from the files:

Actas La Iglesia Metodista en Bolivia, Conferencia Annual Provisional XLII Session Cochabamba, Noviembre 1957.

Actas La Iglesia Metodista en Bolivia, Conferencia Annual Provisional XLIII Session Cochabamba, Noviembre 1958.

Actas Oficiales 1960 XLV Conferencia Annual de La Iglesia Metodista en Bolivia, Cochabamba, Diciembre–Enero 1961.

Actas Oficiales 1961 XLVI Conferencia Annual de La Iglesia Metodista en Bolivia, Cochabamba, Diciembre–Enero 1962.

Arias, Bishop Mortimer. The *Land of a Thousand Faces A Wesleyan Perspective, Christian Mission and Globalization: Mission in Latin America*. Oxford, England: Oxford Institute, 2002.

Boots, Wilson T. *Four Women Confront a Nation*. Christianity and Crisis, May 1, 1978.

Boots, Wilson T. *Reflections on 100 Years of Methodist Witness in Bolivia*, September 2006.

Bloom, Linda. *Bolivian Activist to Receive Methodist Peace Award*. United Methodist News Service, November 14, 2003.

100 Anos Evangelizando Y Sirviendo a Bolivia Celebracion Liturgica Acto de Condecoracion Centenario de la IEMB 1906–2006 (pamphlet). La Paz, Bolivia. *Programa Centennial 14 al 20 de Agosto, 2006*. Folder, La Paz Bolivia.

Boots, Wilson T., *Bolivian Methodists Celebrate Centennial*. The United Methodist Reporter, September 15, 2006.

Boots, Wilson T., *Commentary: Reflections on 100 Years of Methodism in Bolivia*. United Methodist News Service, September 22, 2006.

Pantelis, Jorge M., *Reflectiones Y Apuntes Sobre la Historia Del Sincretismo Y Katarizacion en La IEMB*, 2010.

Loza, Gustavo. *The Mission of the Methodist Church Becomes a Part of the Fabric of Bolivia*. (English translation by Rev. LeGrand Smith) 2007.

Loza, Gustavo. *The Methodist Church Becomes Part of the Historical Fabric of Bolivia: Through Education of Indigenous Peoples Weaving A Great Multicolored Fabric*, 2007.

# Videos

Documents 290 – 194, Between the Foreign Ministry of Bolivia and the U.S. Department of State, from the files of the U.S. Department of state 1955–101957.

#290 Conversation between Assistant Secretary of State and President Siles, August 12, 1957, Economic Assistance to Bolivia for FY 1958, seven pages.

#291 Conversation between Secretary of State and Manuel Barrau Pelaez, Foreign Minister of Bolivia, October 3, 1957, re.: Nationalization of the Mines, 1 page (over lunch).

#292 Conversation between Manuel Barrau Pelaez, Ambassador Victor Andrade, and Mr. Rubottom, ARA, Mr. Turkel, REA, and Mr. Silverstein OSA Department of State, October 3, 1957, 2 pages.

#293 Conversation Between President Hernan Siles Zuazo; Manuel Barrau, Minister of Foreign Relations; Carlos Morales Guilen, Minister of Defense; the Ambassador; and Dr. Moore and Mr. Bridgett, re: President's Comments on the Current Bolivian Situation, November 17, 1957, 4 pages.

#294 Note from the U.S. Embassy in La Paz to the Bolivian Ministry of Foreign Affairs, reply to the August request for supplemental aid, December 23, 1957, 3 pages.

Documents 147–180, Between the Foreign Ministry and the U.S. Department of State, from the files of the U.S. Department of State from March 1964 through December 21, 1968.

Alliance for Progress and Peace Corps, Office of the Historian, Department of State, 1961–1969.

Kornbluh, Peter, The Death of Che Guevara (Declassified), The National Security Archive Electronic Briefing Book, pages 24.

Document File Provided by Dr. Henry Baker Perry III

Perry, III. Henry B., *Curriculum Vitae,* revised 9/28/2021.

Perry, Henry, Nathan Robison, Dardo Chavez, Orlando Taja, Carolina Hilari, David Shanklin, and John Wyon. *Attaining Health For All Through Community Partnerships' Principles of the Census-based, impact-oriented CBIO) Approach to Primary Health Care Developed in Bolivia, South America.* Social Science and Medicine, 48 (1999): 1053–1067.

Perry, Henry L., David Shanklin, and Dirk G. Schroeder. *Impact of a Community-based Primary Healthcare Programme on Infant and Child Mortality in Bolivia, Journal on Health, Population and Nutrition.* (December 21, 2003): 282–295.

Perry, Henry, Nathan Robison, Dargo Chavez, Orlando Taja, Carolina. *The Census-based impact-oriented Approach: Its Effectiveness in Promoting Child Health in Bolivia, Health Policy and Planning,* Oxford University Press (1998): 140–151.

Chavez, Dardo; Mitma Claure, Hilary Moshman, Nathan C. Robison, Ramiro Llanque, and Henry L. Perry. *Implementing the Census-based, Impact-oriented Approach to Comprehensive Primary Health Care Over Three decades in Montero, Bolivia: 1, Program Description.* Preventive Medicine and Community Health (May 2, 2020): 1–7.

Chavez, Dardo, Mitma Claure, Hilary Moshman, Nathan C. Robison, Ramiro Llanque, and Henry L. Perry. *Implementing the Census-based, Impact-oriented Approach to Comprehensive Primary Health Care Over Three decades in Montero, Bolivia: 2, Program Achievements, including Long-Tern Trends in Mortality of Children and Mothers, Description.* Preventive Medicine and Community Health (May 2, 2020): 1–76.

# Audio Files

David Farah, Wycliffe Translators, Oral History Digital Library, Billy Graham Center, Wheaton College, Wheaton, Illinois, Collection #302.

# Appendix I

# Missionary Personnel from the U.S.

In 1937–38, apparently, three persons were assigned to Bolivia, but only one actually served for three years. Three were assigned, but served two-, three-, and five-year terms only. One was assigned in 1940 and left after three years. In 1941, one missionary arrived and stayed ten years. No one arrived in 1942.

### 1943–1968

| | |
|---|---|
| Murray and Nova Dickson | 1943 |
| Loyde Middleton | 1947 |
| Sarah Middleton | 1952 |
| William (Jack) Robison | 1948 |
| Bill and Martha Kent | 1950 |
| LeGrand and Jayne Smith | 1952 |
| Charles and Ruth McFarren | 1952 |
| Keith and Marilyn Hamilton | 1952 |
| Wilson Boots | 1953 |
| Helen Wilson | 1953 |
| Bill Kent | 1954 |
| Cecil and Mary Tinder | 1955 |
| Robert and Rosa Caufield | 1955 |

| | |
|---|---|
| Bill Jack and Mary Lee Marshall | 1955 |
| Gary and Mary Fritz | 1955 |
| James Jones | 1956 |
| Marilaine Jones | 1956 |
| Rosa Sheirlian | 1956 |
| Virginia Bunn | 1956 |
| Thelma Cooley | 1956 |
| Milton and Ruth Ann Robinson | 1857 |
| Ernestine Harmon | 1957 |
| Edward and Natalie Barber | 1957 |
| James and Evelyn Pace | 1957 |
| Paul and Rachel McCleary | 1957 |
| Robinson & Mary McAden | 1958 |
| Robert & Carmen Gnegy | 1958 |
| John & Wanda Schmitz | 1958 |
| Margaret Toothman | 1958 |
| Rosella Bonorden | 1958 |
| Bill Frank | 1959 |
| Jim & Ellen Palmer | 1959 |
| Richard Sizelove | 1969 |
| David & Carole Adams | 1959 |
| Catherine Rocky | 1959 |
| Gary Cornell | 1959 |
| Louis & Sidney Tatum | 1960 |
| Ernest & Anita Eppley | 1960 |
| Russell & Cecilia Dilley | 1960 |
| Wendell & Ruth Kramer | 1960 |
| Harry & Patricia Peacock | 1960 |
| Joyce Reed | 1960 |
| Steven Smith | 1960 |
| Carl & Julia Williams | 1960 |
| Elizabeth Beale | 1961 |
| Dale Good | 1961 |

| | |
|---|---|
| Adele Phillips | 1961 |
| Richard & Lila Palmiter | 1960 |
| Janice Long | 1961 |
| George & Shirley Toadvine | 1962 |
| Ann Love | 1962 |
| Eloise Beatles | 1962 |
| Karlene Cason | 1962 |
| Donella Barry | 1963 |
| Barbara Caufield | 1963 |
| Shirley Robinson | 1964 |
| Jim Tuttle | 1964 |
| Jim and Jean Alley | 1964 |
| Mary Lou Barbre | 1964 |
| Thorburn & Marjorie Thompson | 1964 |
| Judy Good | 1964 |
| Charles & Jean King | 1965 |
| Herb & Darlus Schoonover | 1965 |
| Fern Jo Kaukonen | 1966 |
| John & Carolyn Hickman | 1966 |
| Linda Maynard | 1966 |
| Jim Perkins | 1966 |
| Jim Hoey | 1966 |
| Patricia Baker | 1966 |
| Joy Holloway | 1966 |
| Larry Thompson | 1966 |
| Hulda Wagener | 1966 |
| Sterling Ward | 1966 |
| Martin & Berdene Martin | 1966 |
| Fred & Hilda Thomas | 1967 |
| Bertha Gulasha | 1967 |
| Gabriel Luriauda y Sra. | 1967 |
| Joanna Neff | 1967 |
| Lindsay & Ann Smith | 1968 |

# Appendix II

## Presidents of Bolivia

| Date assumed | Name | Manner entered office |
|---|---|---|
| April 1940 | Enrique Penaranda | Junta |
| December 1943 | Gualberto Villaroel | Junta |
| July 1946 | Nestor Guillen | Popular Uprising |
| August 1946 | Tomas Monje | Junta |
| March 1947 | Enrique Hertzog | Election |
| October 1949 | Mamerto Urriolagoitia | Election |
| May 1951 | Hugo Ballivian | Junta |
| April 1952 | Victor Paz Estenssoro | Revolt election |
| August 1956 | Hernan Siles Zuazo | Election, MNR |
| August 1960 | Victor Paz Estenssoro | Elected, MNR |
| August 1964 | Victor Paz Estenssoro | Elected, MNR |
| Nov. 3, 1964 | Gen. Rene Barrientos | Coup |
| Nov. 4, 1964 | Gen. Alfredo Ovando C. | Co-president |
| Sept. 26, 1969 | Alfredo Ovando Candia | Coup |
| Oct. 6, 1970 | Military Junta | Coup |
| Oct. 7, 1970 | Gen Juan Jose Torres | Installed by Junta |
| Aug. 21, 1971 | Gen Hugo Banzer | Coup |
| July 21, 1978 | Gen David Padilla | Coup |

# Appendix III

## United States Ambassadors to Bolivia

### 1939–1977

Douglas Jenkins, Envoy Extraordinary and Minister Plenipotentiary, October 26, 1939–October 3, 1941.

Pierre de Lagarde Boal, Ambassador Extraordinary and Plenipotentiary, May 23, 1942–February 5, 1944.

Walter C. Thurston, Ambassador Extraordinary and Plenipotentiary, November 16, 1944–January 3, 1946.

Joseph Flack, Ambassador Extraordinary and Plenipotentiary, July 15, 1946–May 17, 1949.

Irving Florman, Ambassador Extraordinary and Plenipotentiary, February 27, 1950–September 4, 1951.

Edward J. Sparks, Ambassador Extraordinary and Plenipotentiary. June 13, 1952–October 29, 1954.

Gerald A. Drew, Ambassador Extraordinary and Plenipotentiary, December 8, 1954–April 6, 1957.

Philip Bonsal, Ambassador Extraordinary and Plenipotentiary, May 10, 1957–February 6, 1959.

Carl W. Strom, Ambassador Extraordinary and Plenipotentiary, May 4, 1959–May 8, 1961.

Ben S. Stephansky, Ambassador Extraordinary and Plenipotentiary, June 29, 1961–October 15, 1963.

Douglas Henderson, Ambassador Extraordinary and Plenipotentiary, December 7, 1963–August 6, 1968.

Raúl Héctor Castro, Ambassador Extraordinary and Plenipotentiary, September 3, 1968–November 3, 1969.

Ernest V. Siracusa, Ambassador Extraordinary and Plenipotentiary, December 5, 1969–July 30, 1973.

William Perry Stedman, Jr, Ambassador Extraordinary and Plenipotentiary, October 3, 1973–June 23, 1977.

# Appendix IV

## Headlines Stories of World Events of Significance from 1960 through 1969

**1960**
    November    Kennedy elected president of the U.S.

**1961**
    April    Bay of Pigs fiasco Cuba
    August    Berlin wall goes up
    November    16,000 troops sent to Vietnam as advisors

**1962**
    January    Troops sent to Saigon
    April    Bay of Pigs prisoners sentenced: 1,179
    May    Kennedy at height of popularity
    October    Cuban missile crisis

**1963**
    February    Missiles out of Cuba, siloes destroyed.
    June    Kennedy speech at Berlin Wall
    August    Martin Luther King speech: I have a Dream!

| | November | President Kennedy Assassinated! |
| --- | --- | --- |
| | November | Lyndon B. Johnson in augurated president of the U.S. |

### 1964

| | August | LBJ signs Civil Rights Act |
| --- | --- | --- |
| | October | World Olympics in Tokyo |
| | November | LBJ Beats Goldwater by a landslide |
| | December | Martin L. King march in Montgomery A |

### 1965

| | January | Winston Churchill dies |
| --- | --- | --- |
| | February | Martin Luther King assassinated |
| | April | Coup in Dominican Republic Reid Cabral ousted |
| | May | 24,000 troops sent to Vietnam |
| | June | Coup d'état in Algeria |
| | July | 50,000 troops sent to Vietnam |
| | August | John signed Voting Rights Act of 1965 |
| | August | Watts Riots |
| | September | 105,000 troops sent to Vietnam |
| | October | Draft cards burned |
| | November | Coup in the Congo. Mobuto, Chief of Staff |

### 1966

| | January | Julian Bond ejected from Georgia House of Representatives, black member |
| --- | --- | --- |
| | January | 8,000 US troops led fight in Vietnam |
| | April | US troop deaths now greater than Vietnamese |
| | May | Growing opposition to war on campuses |
| | June | James Meredith, civil rights activist, shot in the back |
| | July | Rioting in Chicago, New York, and Cleveland; National Guard called |
| | August | Great Proletarian Revolution in China |

| | September | Civil Rights march clash with National Guard |
|---|---|---|
| | November | California elected Reagan as governor |
| | November | First black elected to the senate from MS in eighty-five years |
| | December | U.S. admits there were civilians killed in Vietnam |

**1967**

| | January | U.S. has the highest weekly causalities of the war |
|---|---|---|
| | January | Astronauts killed in flash fire of Apollo I on the pad |
| | January | China in upheaval; army takes charge |
| | February | LBJ CIA close all secret programs on student groups |
| | April | Greek colonels replace the government |
| | May | Eastern region of Nigeria succeed to become Biafra |
| | June | Israel smashes Arabs in Six-Day War |
| | July | Gen. Westmoreland asked for more troops |
| | August | Thurgood Marshall first black named to Supreme Court |
| | September | Gov. Reagan urges more troops to Vietnam |
| | October | Che Guevara killed in Bolivia |
| | October | Blood poured on draft cards |
| | October | Fr. Daniel Barragan and two others arrested over war |
| | November | Great Britain leave Eden after 126 years |
| | December | 546 arrested in NY for opposition to the war |
| | December | LBJ visits troops in Vietnam |

**1968**

| | January | Guerrillas initiate the Tet Offensive in Vietnam; troops in disarray |
|---|---|---|
| | February | Delta flight skyjacked to Cuba |
| | March | LBJ stuns country, "I won't run." |
| | March | Panama president embattled, impeached; will not quit |
| | April | Martin Luther King assassinated! |

| | |
|---|---|
| April | Rioting in Chicago, Baltimore, Washington, DC, and Cincinnati; Feds, troops, and National Guard sent |
| May | U.S. and Vietnam begin Paris Peace talks |
| May | France paralyzed by protests in factories and offices Sorbonne closed for the first time in 700 years |
| June | Bobby Kennedy assassinated! |
| June | 50,000 march for the poor; tent city in D.C. |
| August | Soviet tanks invade Czechoslovakia |
| August | Democratic convention in Chicago faced anti-war demo |
| August | Nominated Hubert Humphrey for president |
| September | Arthur Ashe won the US Open; first black to win a national tennis match |
| November | Richard Nixon and Spiro Agnew won the election |
| November | LBJ called for the end to the bombing of the North |

## 1969

| | |
|---|---|
| January | Cuban skyjacking becomes an epidemic |
| February | Yasir Arafat leads Palestinian forces |
| March | First flight of the Concorde |
| March | Golda Meir is nation's premier |
| April | Apollo 9 returned safely from ten-day mission |
| May | Ant-war activists seize college campuses |
| June | Nixon orders 25,000 out |
| July | Mankind makes its greatest leap: to the moon |
| August | Thousands overwhelm Woodstock Festival |
| September | Libya King ousted Khadafy in power |
| October | Anti-war protests spread across the U.S. |
| November | 250,000 war protesters in the capital |
| November | 567 massacred at Mylie |
| December | Panama's leader out and in again |
| December 31, 1968 | |

176

# Appendix V

## Electoral History of the MNR

| Election | Party candidate | Votes | % | Result |
|---|---|---|---|---|
| 1947 | Victor Paz E. | 5,194 | 5.5% | Lost |
| 1951 | Victor Paz E. | 54,129 | 41.9% | Annulled |
| 1956 | Hernan Siles Z. | 787,129 | 84.4% | Elected |
| 1960 | Victor Paz E. | 735,619 | 76% | Elected |
| 1964 | Victor Paz E. | 1,114,717 | 97% | Elected |
| 1966 | Victor Andrade | 88,099 | 8.7% | Lost |

In 1951, Victor Paz did had the majority but did not have the plurality of votes required by law. He became president one year later after a revolution.

With the coup by General Barrientos in 1964, the MNR was out of power for twelve years.

# Appendix VI

## Immigration to Bolivia

According to the 2001 census, 87,338 of the Bolivian resident population were born outside Bolivia, representing 1.06 percent of the total Bolivian resident population.

| Place | Country | 2001 | 1992 |
|---|---|---|---|
| 1 | Argentina | 27,094 | 17,829 |
| 2 | Brazil | 14,428 | 8,586 |
| 3 | Mexico | 9,377 | 6,607 |
| 4 | Peru | 8,824 | 5,805 |
| 5 | Spain | 5,650 | 1,337 |
| 6 | Chile | 4,163 | 3,909 |

| | | | |
|---|---|---|---|
| 7 | United States | 3,216 | 2,503 |
| 8 | Paraguay | 3,201 | 955 |
| 9 | Canada | 1,635 | 1,435 |
| 10 | Japan | 1,387 | 1,159 |
| 11 | Germany | 1,281 | 1,099 |
| 12 | Colombia | 1,244 | 529 |
| 13 | Belize | 939 | 806 |
| 14 | Italy | 734 | 718 |
| 15 | Ecuador | 652 | N/D |
| 16 | China | 533 | N/D |
| | Other countries | 7,180 | 6,530 |
| **TOTAL** | | **91,538** | **59,807** |

Source: CEPAL[1]

# Appendix VII

## Population Growth

Population in 2021    over 11,200,000

| Year | Population | Growth Rate |
|------|------------|-------------|
| 2022 | 11,992,656 |             |
| 1968 | 4,297,517  | 2.11%       |
| 1965 | 4,038,872  | 2.05%       |
| 1960 | 3,656,955  | 1.95%       |
| 1955 | 3,331,036  | 1.74%       |
| 1950 | 3,081,830  | 0.00%       |

# About the Author

The author shares how the trajectory of life was changed by a single encounter and the ramifications that produced. The author assumed when he enrolled in seminary his future would probably involve being a pastor of a church in rural downstate Illinois. A visit to the seminary by a Methodist bishop from Latin America became an encounter which changed entirely the direction of his career from that of a local church pastor to missionary.

The McCleary family arrived in Bolivia in the last decade before Methodism transitioned from being a mission to becoming a national autonomous church. The author shares the challenges of contributing to the formation of a new church in a developing country struggling to find its new identity.

The view of open country churches visible over the cornfields of Central Illinois, which he served as a student pastor, stands in sharp contrast to living in the poorest country in South America; a country second only to Haiti as the poorest in the Western Hemisphere. Methodism's footing in Bolivia came through the fact that at the turn of the century the Bolivian president had a daughter who was sent to Santiago, Chile, to gain a high school education not yet available to girls in Bolivia.

The author's real education, even after a degree from college and seminary, came from Bolivia. Living among the poor, ministering to families with children is a quick course in understanding how conditions of absolute poverty shapes the world in which many people live. As incongruitous at it may seem, the country was rich in natural resources whose benefit failed to trickle down to improve the daily lives of the indigenous majority of society.

As the author quickly learned, as insignificant as Bolivia appeared, it was an attractive pawn in the larger context of global politics. The expansion of Nazism took easy rootage in the Bolivian quest for an alternative social order different from the past. The end of World War II in Europe only served to scatter the seed to other corners of the world. There were attempts to continue it in countries such as Bolivia. Klaus Barbie was a resident in Bolivia under protective cover offered by lenient military administrations. The emergence of a Cuban presence led by Che Guevarra was an effort to establish a colony in the more insolated eastern area of Bolivia and was another political influence.

The author shares how new theological currents were also influencing the Christian faith as an outgrowth of conditions in Latin America. These new challenges came in the form of liberation theology articulated by Gustavo Gutierrez, and identification with the poor by Paulo Freire were also gaining wider acceptance.

The author was so influenced by these ten years in Bolivia, he went on to direct three different international non-profit organizations which focus on combating the conditions of absolute poverty on children and families. In so doing, he served as staff of the National Council of Churches, on commissions of the World Council of Churches, as president of the Non-Governmental Organizations Committee to UNICEF, and as member of the Bishops' Task Force on Children and Poverty of the United Methodist Church.